# THE 'DARK' AGES

# THE 'DARK' AGES

## FROM THE SACK OF ROME TO HASTINGS

MARTIN J. DOUGHERTY

amber
BOOKS

Copyright © 2019 Amber Books Ltd

Published by Amber Books Ltd
United House
London N7 9DP
United Kingdom
www.amberbooks.co.uk
Instagram: amberbooksltd
Facebook: www.facebook.com/amberbooks
Twitter: @amberbooks

Project Editor: Sarah Uttridge
Designer: Brian Rust
Picture Research: Terry Forshaw

ISBN: 978-1-78274-903-5

Printed in China

# CONTENTS

QVANTA STRA
GE VIRVM SVBLI
MIS ALEXIA CESSIT
CÆSAREIS AQVI
LIS. PICTA TABEL
LA NOTAT

# INTRODUCTION

The term 'Dark Age' has connotations of chaos, barbarism and wanton violence; a time in which states collapsed rather than prospered and life was a miserable struggle for survival. This view of the period following the fall of the Western Roman Empire has been challenged for many years but remains strangely persistent.

THE 'Dark Ages' of Europe represent a vaguely defined era between the fall of Rome and the emergence of medieval kingdoms, overlapping various more precisely defined periods. There were also local variations; at any given time, civilization might be flowering in one region while another was consumed in war or suffering plague and famine. Overall, the so-called Dark Ages can be considered to begin with the collapse of the Western Roman Empire and to end with the emergence of the Norman kingdom in Britain.

Dark Ages have descended upon many cultures over the centuries, notably the Greek Dark Age. This lasted around 400

OPPOSITE: **This 1533 depiction of the Roman siege of Alesia imposes contemporary clothing and equipment on the Gauls and their enemies. The Romans fight under the German double-headed eagle flag, perhaps implying an inheritance of Rome's glory and status.**

ABOVE: The fall of Mycenae was part of a wider chain of disasters that engulfed the eastern Mediterranean around 1200 BC. Little is known about the resulting 'Greek Dark Age', other than that population numbers dropped sharply and cities were abandoned.

years from the fall of Mycenae in 1200 BC and was part of the wider Bronze Age Collapse in which several other societies were destroyed. Very little is known about this period as virtually no records have survived, but it is clear that civilization around the eastern Mediterranean was wracked by a period of warfare and political turmoil.

In ancient Greece and the Mediterranean there is evidence of the systematic destruction of one coastal city after another. Populations were greatly reduced and entire regions were all but abandoned. The collapse was so total that what came before is recalled only as heroic legend and myth derived from oral histories or perhaps invented tales. The European 'Dark Ages' were mild by comparison.

It is perhaps reasonable to use the term 'dark age' for an era in which literacy was low and from which relatively few writings have survived. However, this does not correlate to an era of chaos and violence. It is true that after the fall of the Roman Empire Europe was less civilized, or at least far less organized, than it had been. There was indeed a great deal of conflict and destruction, and whole cultures were uprooted by traumatic events.

Yet at the same time the post-Roman states of Europe were establishing a new order or continuing the Roman one – albeit with a local flavour – as best they could. Kingdoms were emerging that would be the foundation of our modern states. Explorers would find new lands in distant seas and colonize them, while traders established links with Africa and the Far East.

Great works were also undertaken and bodies of law were written. The people who built St Hilda's Abbey at Whitby in AD 657 were not struggling to survive another day amid a torrent of barbarism, and those who attended the Synod there in AD 664 were sufficiently assured of their future that they felt able to debate how to calculate the correct date to celebrate Easter.

## THE PRE-ROMAN WORLD

It is natural to consider the light of civilization diminished with the collapse of the Roman Empire. At its height the empire stretched from one end of the Mediterranean to the other, and far beyond. It created a unified system for trade, defence and the rule of law. Of course, it was flawed. Internal corruption and the sheer distances involved meant that the empire was less unified than a casual observer might imagine. However, the stabilizing force of Rome permitted exploration, learning and trade on a previously unimaginable scale.

Before the rise of the Roman Empire, Europe was fragmented into countless city states and tribal regions. Conflict between them was inevitable, but by no means constant. Most tribes got along well enough most of the time and long-distance trade did occur. Distance was a greater barrier in this era, however, since travelling meant passing through the territory of many small states and tribes, each of which would have its own agenda. A conflict anywhere on a trader's route was disruptive and, lacking the protection of a nearby powerful state, an expedition would be vulnerable.

BELOW: A bas-relief from Trier in Germany depicting trade in cloth and leather. Commerce was both facilitated by a stable Roman Empire and essential to its continued existence.

The concept of nation states in the modern sense did not exist in the pre-Roman world and local divisions were more important than general similarities. The people of Athens and Sparta were all Greeks, but their loyalty was to their city and perhaps its allies. An attack on a non-allied Greek city state might not matter or could even be seen as beneficial if it weakened a rival. Likewise, the tribes of northern Europe might have been labelled 'Gauls' or 'Celts' but there was no unity among them beyond what was created by their tribal alliances.

It was this disunity that allowed Rome, initially at the head of a republic of allied cities and later as an imperial power, to conquer and dominate Europe and the Middle East. Tribes and city states might jointly fight against Roman incursions but they were not a unified force with organized logistics and a formal command structure. Most importantly, their alliances were generally transient and today's co-belligerent might well be tomorrow's aggressor. The expansion of Rome was opposed on a piecemeal basis by those who felt they had to fight. Others were co-opted by economic means or bowed to the inevitable.

## ROMAN UNITY

For all its flaws and internal conflicts, the Roman Empire brought stability to most areas most of the time, allowing increased prosperity through trade and the establishment of a common language. Greater resources could be brought to bear on a problem than by a tribe or city state, allowing hard times to be weathered and great works to be accomplished. Learning and the sharing of knowledge could also flourish in a more stable environment.

At its height, the Roman Empire might have seemed unassailable and the Romanization of all Europe inevitable as a result of retired soldiers being granted land and money saved from their pay. These rich and experienced men employed others in their households and created the beginnings of a unified European culture based on Roman values and funded by Roman coins. Yet the empire fell, leaving behind a power

BELOW: Much of what we know about the ancient world comes from Roman writings. Without the education system of a powerful empire, less was written about the events of the post-Roman world outside of religious institutions.

LEFT: An 1847 depiction of Roman decadence. With civilization came the possibility of a safe life characterized by indolence and hedonism. Once decadence outweighed energy, the Roman Empire was doomed.

vacuum and an age of wandering tribes harassed by invaders from the east. Small wonder, then, that historians compare the difficult times of the 'Dark Ages' unfavourably with the flawed greatness of Rome. It must have seemed to some at least that they were indeed living in a dark age. The light of Rome had been extinguished and only flickering candles remained to replace it.

By the end of this Dark Age, however, great kingdoms had emerged. Christianity had spread across Europe and great cathedrals were being built to the glory of God. The states of the medieval period would eventually become the nations of today. It might be better to think of this period not as a 'dark age' but as a period of transition, in which the ancient world was swept away and replaced with the beginnings of the modern.

# 1

# THE ROMAN ERA

It is difficult to say when the decline of the Roman Empire began or when its fall became inevitable. It has been suggested that the beginning of the end may have been as early as the reign of Emperor Hadrian (AD 117–138). It was at Hadrian's behest that permanent fortifications were built around the fringes of the empire, signalling an end to the era of expansion.

ALL EMPIRES go through an early, expansionistic phase followed by a period of consolidation that can become stagnation. Crises are inevitable and can actually prolong the life of an empire. The surge of effort required to overcome a challenge, and the outpouring of new ideas that accompanies it, can reinvigorate the empire and give it a new lease of life.

What appears to be a golden age of peace and prosperity can in some cases be a loss of drive and energy, with the empire dozing in comfortable middle age while younger, more vibrant societies arise on its borders. There is also a tendency to stop looking outward and to become more concerned with personal

OPPOSITE: The fall of Rome is often seen as the moment the 'light of civilization' went out in Western Europe. This concept owes much to the idealized vision of the Classical world that emerged much later; the reality of the time was more complex.

ABOVE: Hadrian's Wall in northern Britannia made the most of natural features to create a formidable barrier. Its construction was an admission that the lands to the north could not be conquered.

advancement and internal power plays. A crisis at the right time can result in a new wave of expansion, reorganization or simply a refocus on external matters, all of which can delay the inevitable decline and fall of an empire. The same threat, at a time when the empire is fragmented, can cause a sudden and catastrophic collapse.

## THE GROWTH OF AN EMPIRE

Early in the history of the Roman Republic, the tribes along its borders were a threat to its very survival. They never ceased to be, but over time the people of Rome became more assured of their dominance. There were careers to be made fighting the foes of the empire, but the average citizen in AD 150 did not fear a repeat of 390 BC, when an army of Gauls sacked Rome itself.

The crises faced by the early republic forced innovation and growth. The Roman Army changed its weapons and tactics after the sacking of Rome in 390 BC. The First Punic War, fought against Carthage (264–241 BC), required the creation of a navy. Threats of an incursion by Gauls into Italy forced social changes that created the classic Roman Army, and required reforms in its training and fighting methods under Gaius Marius (157–86 BC).

These and other crises shaped the political and military thinking of the Roman state, creating the army and navy that became the tools of the empire. Some conquests were made out of necessity, and in other cases areas were annexed more or less peacefully. Much of Rome's expansion, however, was fuelled by the personal ambition of individuals.

The most graphic example of this is of course Gaius Julius Caesar, who engineered a dispute with nearby Gallic tribes in order to undertake a campaign of conquest. His intention was to use war to enrich himself – or rather to dig himself out of the financial hole he had dug with lavish spending to support his

BELOW: **The First Punic War (264–241 BC) required innovation to avoid defeat. They were not natural mariners, but the Romans were able to break Carthaginian naval power, turning the tide of the war.**

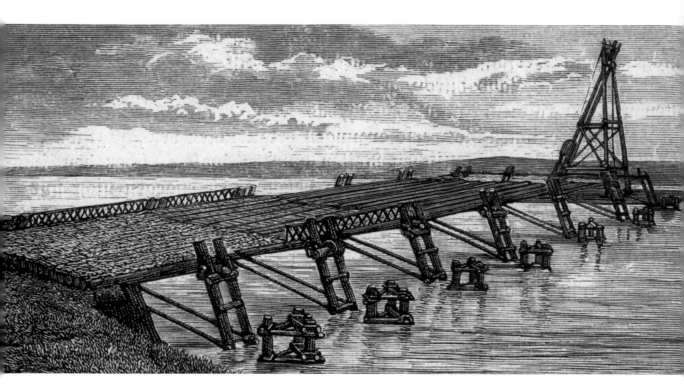

ABOVE: Bridging the Rhine was an impressive but unnecessary achievement. By this point, Julius Caesar was essentially showboating to gain status in Rome rather than defending its interests.

political ambitions. Although successful, he decided not to stop and continued his campaigns in Gaul. Many of his actions were needless and in some cases a pretext was cynically engineered.

Caesar's adventures included bridging the Rhine and even launching a brief foray into Britain, but most importantly he established himself as a great military and political leader – the two were intertwined in Roman society – with the support of an experienced army. When Caesar returned to Italy his political

## CROSSING THE RUBICON

JULIUS CAESAR WAS SUMMONED to Rome, but bringing his army with him across the Rubicon into Italy was forbidden. Interpreting the situation as a gambit to separate him from the protection and support of his troops, he decided to commit an act of treason rather than make himself helpless among his enemies. Conflict became inevitable at that point. Had Caesar gone meekly to Rome as ordered, he might have been quietly done away with and history would have taken a very different turn.

enemies fled, leaving him in control of the capital during a civil war that ultimately established him as sole ruler.

Julius Caesar was not the first emperor of Rome in name, but his actions changed the republic into an empire and also set the tone for Roman politics thereafter. Powerful men with the backing of the army – or enough of it to defeat their rivals – could challenge for the imperial throne. Campaigns against outsiders might be fought out of necessity, but they could also be tools in the power plays that really mattered: the struggle for control of the empire.

The manner in which the Roman Empire came into being established both its great strength and its main weakness. Rome's powerful army was an effective tool in the hands of driven, ambitious men, but it could be directed inward just as easily as outward. When the ambitions of emperors were outward, Rome would grow; when internal conflict consumed the attention of the ruling elite, threats on the borders might grow unchecked.

## PAX ROMANUM

The strength of the Roman Empire enabled it to impose a period of relative peace and stability within its territory. This 'Pax Romanum' is generally considered to have lasted from around AD 27 to AD 180.

BELOW: **Julius Caesar was never emperor as such, but his name became synonymous with rulership. As late as the twentieth century, the Tsar of Russia and the Kaiser of Germany derived their titles from Caesar's name.**

# THE EVOLUTION OF THE ROMAN ARMY

THE ROMAN ARMY INITIALLY used a similar model to the forces of the contemporary Greek city states. The primary striking force was made up of hoplites – heavy infantry armed with long spears who fought in close order. A citizen had to provide his own arms and armour, so at this time warfare was mainly a matter for the upper echelons of society. Lesser citizens served as lightly armed supporting troops.

This model was adequate when Rome was a city state, although the hoplite force it could field was not well suited to the mountainous Italian terrain. As a result the organization of the infantry evolved, eventually leading to the manipular legion. Instead of fighting as an inflexible phalanx, the new legions were subdivided into maniples that could undertake independent manocuvres.

A legion was a force of about 4200 infantry supported by its own cavalry and light infantry, creating a flexible combined-arms force capable of dealing with most threats. The superiority of this new arrangement was demonstrated in a series of victories over Greek forces using the phalanx. Initially, the third line of each maniple – composed of the most experienced men – retained the long spear while the first two lines fought with sword and javelin. Eventually, all Roman infantry came to be armed with the gladius and pilum.

The manipular system worked well, but it required a greater level of training than a phalanx or a horde of unorganized warriors. As Rome's power increased, the demands on its military class became ever greater, with landowners and businessmen away on campaign for years at

LEFT: The Roman soldier's primary advantage over 'barbarian' enemies was a sophisticated system of tactics allowing mutual support and the relief of tired men fighting in the front lines.

a time. The economic damage weakened the republic and eventually forced a set of radical reforms.

One of the most important changes was the provision of arms and armour by the state rather than the individual, opening up military service to a larger segment of society and ensuring that the burden of service no longer fell primarily upon the most economically productive citizens. Reforms also created a professional soldier class whose members benefited from long experience and formalized training. At the same time, lessons were learned about supporting the army in the field and moving forces over long distances. The legions lost their organic cavalry and light infantry elements and were instead supported by auxiliary troops organized as separate formations.

ABOVE: The organization of a legion permitted complex battlefield manoeuvres, but required a well-trained professional force if these were not to disintegrate into chaos.

In later years, service in the legions was a route to full Roman citizenship for those born outside of Italy. Twenty-five years of service were required, but at the end a man was set up for life with citizenship, land and money. The army that won Rome an empire was a professional fighting force in an era of warriors and citizen-soldiers, and it was supported by an effective logistics network that simply did not exist elsewhere. It was organization, training and well-planned logistics as much as the swords of the legionaries that defeated Rome's enemies.

The peace was not universal, of course, but an efficient system of governorship and the ability to rapidly move military forces into an area ensured that rebellions were short-lived and incursions from outside the empire were quickly dealt with.

The Roman Empire reached its greatest extent in AD 117. At this time, its military system was in its classic form: legions of heavy infantry supported by auxiliary regiments fulfilling specialist functions such as light infantry, cavalry and archers. Legions raised in one province served in another, reducing the chance of troops sympathizing with a local rebellion. Retired soldiers became landowners and businessmen in the lands where they had served, creating a Romanizing influence that might one day have led to a unified European culture.

EARTH AND WOOD WERE REPLACED WITH STONE; THE FOCUS TURNED INWARD RATHER THAN OUTWARD. POWER WITHIN THE EMPIRE BECAME MORE IMPORTANT THAN INCREASING THE POWER OF THE EMPIRE.

The empire was threatened by crises and conflicts during this period, as it had during its early expansion. However, this was the era of greatest strength and, more importantly, unity. Crises were tests that strengthened and reinvigorated the empire rather than threatening to destroy it and, despite setbacks on the frontiers, the future of the empire seemed assured.

Perhaps the people of Rome were a little too assured of their future or perhaps the empire had simply grown too large to be effectively governed even by the efficient Roman state. Temporary fortifications along the borders became permanent as earth and wood were replaced with stone; the focus turned inward rather than outward. Power within the empire became more important than increasing the power of the empire.

## YEARS OF DECLINE

The last of the 'Five Good Emperors', Marcus Aurelius, died in AD 180, a date considered to be the end of the Pax Romanum. His successor, Commodus, inherited a period of peace and stability but his reign was beset by plots and conspiracies. After his assassination in AD 192, civil war broke out, resulting in the 'Year of Five Emperors'.

# ROMAN SWORDS

THE ROMAN LEGIONS ARE famously associated with the gladius hispaniensis, the 'Spanish sword' derived from the weapons of the Celtiberians. However, they started out using a Greek-style weapon with a heavy cutting blade and eventually replaced the gladius with a longer sword more suited to cutting strokes, much like the weapons of the 'barbarian' people the legions faced. By the late Roman era, troops were often equipped with their tribal weapons with no real attempt to provide uniform equipment to all legions across the empire.

The strength of the empire was drained by corruption as well as strife. The Praetorian Guard, supposedly bodyguards to the emperor, demanded increasingly huge bribes and acted as kingmakers – more or less openly inviting bids from political figures who wanted to be the next emperor.

The Roman Army underwent significant changes during this period. Legions were increasingly deployed in static positions along the borders, detaching elements to deal with problems elsewhere. The younger and more vigorous members of a legion were sent marching to trouble zones while the older and less fit men remained in defensive deployments. These frontier units naturally underwent a decline in efficiency compared to their forebears, not least since their mindset was defensive and they were not hardened by constant aggressive rushing around as earlier legions would have been. However, the border forces were for the most part effective and

BELOW: The murderous insanity of Emperor Commodus resulted in his assassination at the hands of an expert wrestler, who strangled him.

were able to call upon reinforcements from other provinces or areas deeper within the empire.

It became standard practice to recruit troops from outside the empire. Service in an auxiliary regiment did not grant citizenship, but earned the right for the soldier's sons to serve in a Roman legion, which did. The system of military service for citizenship continued to produce good-quality recruits for the army, although as time went on there was an increased 'barbarization' of the Roman Army. Barbarization in this case meant a departure from the neatly organized and uniformly equipped legions as the backbone of the army, in favour of formations equipped in the native fighting style of their recruits. This was a useful expedient, especially since cavalry was supplanting infantry as the main striking arm of the Roman Army. Rather than mould recruits to the Roman way, it became increasingly common to make use of the talents they already had.

By the late 200s AD, the empire was weak and divided. Years of internal conflict and power struggles had eroded the cohesion of the empire, impeding any attempt to respond to a crisis. The need to maintain large armies to fight against incursions and against fellow Romans drained a treasury no longer swollen with plunder from conquered lands, and still politicians spent vast sums on defeating one another's schemes rather than solving the empire's problems.

The defensive strategy depended on a hard outer crust of defended regions, but if this were penetrated the invaders could run riot until a cohesive response finally emerged. This was by no means guaranteed

BELOW: The Praetorian Guard enjoyed many privileges, including a shorter term of service than the common legionaries. There was also the possibility of extorting huge sums of money out of imperial candidates.

to happen at all and many cities were plundered towards the end of the third century. The result was essentially a military coup, although Roman politics and military matters were so intertwined that arguably any scheme by a powerful man was effectively military in nature.

THE SYSTEM OF MILITARY SERVICE FOR CITIZENSHIP CONTINUED TO PRODUCE GOOD-QUALITY RECRUITS FOR THE ARMY.

## TWO EMPIRES

In AD 284, Diocletian was proclaimed emperor with the backing of the military. This temporarily improved the situation, but a long-term solution was needed. Diocletian divided the Roman world into the Eastern and Western Roman Empires, ruled from Byzantium and Rome respectively, in the hope that each region would be more governable and that the whole would prosper.

The experiment was not a great success, and Diocletian's abdication in AD 305 was followed by a period of civil war. From this emerged Emperor Constantine, last ruler of a unified Roman Empire. After him, the empire was again divided. Constantine also embraced Christianity, whose adherents had previously been persecuted. This made Christianity the official state religion of the empire, though not without resistance.

The Eastern Roman Empire, with its capital renamed Constantinople, charted its own path after the divide. It became a player in the politics of medieval Europe and the Middle East, and briefly attempted to restore the Western Roman Empire. As the Byzantine Empire, the Eastern Roman Empire survived until 1453, at which point Europe was experiencing the first stirrings of what would become the Renaissance. The Western Roman Empire, on the other hand, was destined for collapse and conquest.

## HUN INCURSIONS

The origins of the people known as Huns are not known for sure. It has been speculated that they originated far to the east in Asia and migrated westwards over many

BELOW: Emperor Diocletian tried to end years of internal strife by creating a system of four rulers rather than a single emperor.

DIOCLETIANVS

# ROMAN CAVALRY

IN THE EARLY HISTORY of Rome, legions included a body of 300 cavalry, drawn from the upper echelons of society. This number was later doubled. The inclusion of cavalry gave the early legion a mobile striking element, but the decisive blow was struck by the much larger body of infantry.

Over time, this cavalry element was phased out and replaced by cavalry from the auxilia regiments, with all members of a legion being infantry. The cavalry formed a separate force, organized as alae, or wings. Despite being more numerous than previously, cavalry were mainly used for screening, scouting and as flank guards.

As the army of the empire became more static and defensively minded, cavalry detachments were used to patrol between the fortified areas of the border and to deal with incursions or small rebellions. By this time the equipment of the Roman Army varied considerably from one unit to the next, but typically a cavalry force would be armed with several light throwing spears and a sword. This was commonly a spatha, much longer than the gladius hispaniensis traditionally associated with the infantry.

In fact, infantry also moved to longer swords over time.

Some cavalry used lances rather than throwing spears, and most were armoured in scale or mail coats with additional protection from helmets and shields. The clibanarii and cataphractii deployed by the Eastern Roman Empire were much more heavily protected, but in the West cavalry were armoured more lightly.

Over time these armoured horsemen, often raised from 'barbarian' peoples rather than civilized Roman provinces, became the main striking arm of the Roman Army. The infantry remained important but it was the cavalry who could chase down an incursion or overwhelm a raiding party, and on the battlefield the Roman cavalry increased in prowess.

By the time of the fall of the Western Roman Empire, cavalry were seen as the main combat force in most regions and being a mounted soldier was an indication of high social status. Arguably, the dominance of Europe by the mounted 'knight' began in the latter days of the Roman Empire.

decades. They are mentioned in Roman sources starting in AD 91, where they are stated to live near the Caspian Sea in what is now Kazakhstan.

At the end of the first century, the Huns were not much of a threat to Rome – no barbarian tribe or coalition of tribes really

was. They were far away, beyond the lands of other tribes, and not powerful enough to challenge the Roman legions. Roman sources of the time are vague about the identities of many tribes – probably because their writers lacked clear information – and tend to refer to the people of a region using sweeping generalizations. In the case of the Caspian Sea region, the common term was Scythians.

Tribal coalitions formed and broke up over time, sometimes conquering many other tribes to attain great, if temporary, power. At times, tribes that were not closely related might be part of a confederation, and at others related tribes might be part of different groupings. The tribal confederations known to the Romans and other outsiders were thus political rather than necessarily implying shared biological or even cultural heritage.

One of the major tribal groupings of the late fourth century was the Alans, who probably originated in the Caspian/Aral Sea region. They had been known to the Romans for many years and were for a time considered the best cavalry in the world. Alan

ABOVE: **As the Huns overran enemies such as the Alans, they co-opted their warriors for further conquests. Those that were not subjugated were driven west, where they caused great disruption.**

mercenaries served many masters and as a political entity they had warred against the Sassanid dynasty in Persia and fought both with and against the Parthians.

The Alan confederation was disrupted by Gothic tribes moving into the area, leading to the establishment of an eastern Alan region on the Danube and a western region on the Don. This may have been one of the factors that allowed the Huns to rise to prominence. Some Alans sided with the Huns whereas others fought against them. The Huns were victorious, overrunning lands previously owned by the Alans and driving them westwards.

The Alans and the Huns both favoured a highly aggressive and mobile form of warfare, making use of the bow from horseback. The traditional Roman legion was not well suited to battling such foes, as previous campaigns had shown. As early as 53 BC Crassus, a contemporary of Julius Caesar, led a Roman Army to destruction at the hands of Parthian cavalry in the region of Carrhae.

THE ALANS AND HUNS BOTH FAVOURED A HIGHLY AGGRESSIVE AND MOBILE FORM OF WARFARE, MAKING USE OF THE BOW FROM HORSEBACK.

The Roman Army of AD 370 was quite different to that commanded by Crassus. Less uniformly equipped but containing far more cavalry, it was at least capable of matching the Huns in terms of mobility. More importantly, the Roman Empire had begun creating buffer zones against incursions by allowing displaced tribes to settle within the borders of the empire.

The Goths of the Crimea were pushed westwards by the Hun invasion and were granted permission to settle along the Danube in return for service as foederati. Foederati were not Roman citizens, but were expected to defend the areas they were granted. Thus the empire gained the service of ferocious 'barbarian' warriors to protect its interior, at a stroke increasing its defensive capabilities and eliminating the threat from the wandering tribe.

This could be an effective ploy, but only if relations with the foederati remained good. There was little chance of this if they were mistreated by the Roman provincial governors and, shortly after settling along the Danube, the Goths began to rebel. A series of small battles escalated into a major crisis, causing Emperor Valens to muster what forces he could to crush the revolt. In AD 378 Valens's force confronted the infantry of the Goths near Adrianople while their cavalry were away, but the emperor wasted the opportunity to launch a decisive attack. Instead, his hesitant advance was repelled long enough for the Gothic cavalry to return and rout the Roman Army.

The battle of Adrianople has been put forward by some historians as the point where cavalry supplanted infantry as the main combat arm in European warfare, setting the tone for the next few centuries. Be that as it may, Emperor Valens was killed at Adrianople and his army suffered heavy losses, further draining the empire's military manpower. One consequence of this defeat was an even greater reliance on foederati rather than Roman troops – at this point, the Western Roman Empire was protected by warriors who bore only the most superficial resemblance to the legionaries of previous centuries.

ABOVE: After their victory at Adrianople, the Goths advanced on Constantinople, threatening the capital of the Eastern Empire before a new emperor was selected. Their attack was unsuccessful, forcing the Goth Army to withdraw.

## ALARIC TAKES ROME

Little is known about the early life of Alaric, king of the Visigoths. It seems that he was born around AD 370, presumably into a powerful family. Like many 'barbarian' leaders of the time, he served the Roman Empire as a commander and eventually a general, leading forces raised from his own people. Alaric fought in Roman internal conflicts between Emperor Theodosius and Flavius Eugenius, who had taken the throne of the Western Roman Empire. Eugenius requested but was refused recognition

# INFANTRY VS CAVALRY

THE ROMAN LEGION WAS an excellent fighting force, but it was best suited to defeating enemies who fought on foot. If enemy horsemen preferred to use hand weapons, the legionaries could wait in a defensive formation and strike back with pilum and gladius when the enemy closed, but against horse archers the legion was at a severe disadvantage.

This led to defeats at the hands of enemies such as the Parthians. The legion required the support of auxiliary or allied cavalry against opponents who possessed superior mobility, but these forces rarely possessed the reliability of the legions. At the battle of Carrhae in 53 BC, a large Roman force was utterly defeated by Parthian horsemen who drove off the supporting cavalry and then wore down the legions without coming to handstrokes. As incursions by the Huns and other mounted people increased, the Roman Empire had to make increasing use of its own cavalry.

ABOVE: An anachronistic depiction of Alaric, king of the Visigoths, wearing articulated plate armour that would not be invented for several centuries.

by Theodosius, the last Roman to rule a united empire. Instead, Theodosius set out to crush the usurper, and included large numbers of Gothic warriors in his army.

Alaric's Goths suffered heavy casualties at the Battle of River Frigidus in AD 394 and Alaric felt that his people had been cynically sacrificed to spare Roman lives. However, the Goths were bound by a treaty that allowed them to live in the Balkans as foederati but required military service without the benefits of citizenship. After the death of Theodosius, Alaric attempted to renegotiate the treaty. When diplomacy failed, he launched a campaign of pillage across the Balkans, sacking several towns and cities to underline his point that Rome needed the protection of his people.

This led to a deal whereby Alaric would ally with the Western Roman Empire and conquer the east. It seems likely that the deal was made in good faith, but incursions from Gaul and other threats made it impossible to send forces or the money Alaric demanded in return for being forced to wait around. When neither was forthcoming, the Goths reverted to strong-arm tactics and began moving westwards towards Italy.

The Western Roman Empire considered this a threat and mustered forces to counter it, incidentally massacring potential allies of Alaric's Goths. This triggered a mutiny and additional forces that might have opposed Alaric went over to his cause. The Goths sacked numerous cities on their way to Rome, though notably bypassed Ravenna, which was at the time the capital of the Western Roman Empire.

Alaric besieged Rome and demanded tribute, but still wanted to negotiate with the empire. Rather than assault the city, he held it hostage in the hope that Ravenna would see reason. Despite some token diplomacy, the Western Empire resolved to chase the 'barbarians' out of Italy and sent forces to raise the siege. These were easily seen off by the Goths.

Alaric eventually lost patience and sacked Rome before marching his army onwards towards Sicily. He had not come to Italy as a conqueror so much as to obtain a favourable

BELOW: The fall of Rome to Alaric and the Visigoths was, despite the drama depicted here, something of a historical damp squib. Alaric did not set out to conquer the city, and the Western Roman Empire made little effort to defend it.

OPPOSITE: Medieval images of Attila say more about the culture that created them than the man they supposedly depict. Attila would not have styled himself as a medieval western European monarch.

bargaining position. With the empire unwilling to negotiate even for its spiritual home, there was no more Alaric could do. He died in AD 410 and his successor, Athaulf, decided to march into Gaul. Although Alaric did not live to see it, his aim was finally achieved – the Goths created themselves a new homeland in Gaul where they were no longer beholden to the Romans. As for the empire, it could not recover from the twin blows of losing the Goths as foederati and the damage they did on their march to their new home.

## FURTHER HUN CONQUESTS

The leader of the Huns, Rugila, died in AD 433 leaving his nephews Bleda and Attila in command. Although almost universally referred to as 'the Huns', their forces included warriors from many cultures including Goths, Alemanni and Alans. Some of these were similar to the Huns in their use of cavalry, but Hunnish armies included large contingents of warriors who normally fought on foot. They also incorporated siege weapons to break the defences of towns.

The Huns appear to have been more adept than their Roman opponents at making use of warriors from other cultures and perhaps treated them more fairly. That, and the fact that the Huns were fearsome enemies but generous overlords, for the most part kept allied tribes from switching sides. The threat of the huge Hun Army was sufficient that they were able to extort huge bribes from the Roman authorities; treaties in AD 435 and 439 guaranteed tribute to the Huns in return for them seeking other targets.

It may be that the Roman authorities thought they had made a good deal; in return for large payments the Huns agreed to defend the Danube region, freeing Roman troops for use elsewhere. Using barbarians in this manner was a typical Roman stratagem of the time and indeed the Huns had previously served as mercenaries in Roman power struggles. For a time the Huns turned their attention elsewhere, notably against Sassanian Persia, which must have further pleased Roman officials. Two potential enemies fighting one another could only be a good thing.

By this time, Rome was facing yet another crisis. Weakened by warfare and plague, its forces desperately needed rebuilding but the funds to support expansion were simply not available. Weakness invited rebellion, further draining manpower, and allowed external challenges to be successful. The Vandals, who had established a power base in North Africa, captured the Roman province of Carthage. This threatened the food supply of Rome itself, as Carthage had become a critical supplier of grain and other foodstuffs.

A response was absolutely necessary and to provide the necessary troops the Roman authorities pulled legions out of what seemed like less critically threatened areas such as the Balkans. This was too tempting for the Huns, who announced that their treaty with the Roman Empire had not been honoured. An attempt at negotiation came to nothing and in AD 441 the Huns began to sweep through the Balkans, sacking cities as they went.

Despite an attempt to recall forces from elsewhere and halt the Hun advance, city after city was overwhelmed until the Hun Army was within striking range of Constantinople itself. At this point, the empire agreed to pay a greatly increased tribute to avoid destruction and the Huns withdrew. A bought peace rarely lasts, however, and this was no exception.

BELOW: Attila and his warriors are depicted here burning the city of Aquila. Savagery of this sort was a tool of statecraft; cities often chose to surrender peacefully in order to avoid the same fate.

## HUN RULER

Attila became sole ruler of the Huns in AD 445, upon the death of his brother Bleda. There are various theories about his involvement in Bleda's demise, but what is certain is that Attila launched renewed campaigns of conquest after his brother's death. After plundering the Balkans, Attila became embroiled in a situation that ultimately led his forces west.

With a typically Roman perspective, Honoria – the sister of the Western Roman Emperor Valentinian III – tried to elicit Attila's help in avoiding an arranged political marriage. She sent him her engagement ring, which Attila decided was an offer of marriage. He naturally asked for a significant part of the empire as a wedding gift and refused to accept that the intention had been any different. When Valentinian would not do as Attila wanted, the Huns marched west.

Other reasons for the Hunnish invasion of Gaul have been put forward, most of which arise from the complex politics of the time. Attila may have wanted to set up vassal states in Germania and Gaul, or to resolve political problems arising from hosting fugitive members of foreign noble houses at his court. Whether or not Attila's pretext for invasion was to force Rome to honour the marriage proposal he was adamant he had received, he decided to invade Gaul and make war upon the Visigothic kingdom developing around Toulouse.

Such was the state of Roman affairs at that time that Attila's proposed alliance against the Visigoths was seriously considered. They and other tribal groups in Gaul were in varying states of

ABOVE: Attila's invasion of Western Europe was halted at the Battle of the Catalaunian Fields, by an alliance of Roman and Frankish forces. The fact that the Franks were allies and not foederati indicates the degree of Roman weakness at the time.

near-revolt and it was largely a question of when rather than if Rome would need to suppress them. The empire of a century earlier would have dealt with its own problems and dictated a deal to those whose help it wanted, but now Rome was tottering from one crisis to the next.

Survival of the empire depended upon playing threats off against one another, ideally weakening potential rebels in battle against current ones. The decision as to which was the greatest threat was a difficult one, but eventually Rome decided to ally with the Visigoths under their king Theodoric rather than attacking them. A Roman Army under general Flavius Aetius joined forces with the Visigoths and finally defeated the Huns at the Battle of the Catalaunian Fields in AD 451.

Attila's army at that time included forces from conquered tribes including Alans, Gepids and Goths. He had overrun much of northern Europe but was finally defeated not by a Roman Army but by a force of allies that included Rome. It is notable that Flavius Aetius was hesitant about exploiting his victory or supporting the Visigoths too closely. It may be that he hoped Theodoric's forces would be weakened and thus a potential threat to Rome diminished. Be that as it may, Theodoric was killed in the fighting and the Huns were turned back from western Europe.

Attila died soon afterward and the Hun threat dissolved into internal fighting. The Huns retained a power base on the Danube – in what is now Hungary – but ceased to be a major factor in the events unfolding within Europe. However, they had set in motion a chain of events that would see the Western Roman Empire swept away and the beginnings of a new era.

## THE FALL OF THE WESTERN ROMAN EMPIRE

The Western Roman Empire did not collapse for a single reason but as the result of a downward spiral from which there was no escape. Rebellions and invasions not only cost vast sums to deal with but disrupted the economy that should have raised this money. Provinces that were not recovered and restored to prosperity resulted in reduced revenue, and military weakness meant having to pay bribes to obtain short-term peace, further draining the imperial coffers.

Some barbarian people from outside the empire, or who had settled within it, saw Roman weakness as a chance to plunder the cities and trade routes. Others marched into Roman territory seeking a new home. In some cases this was simple opportunism, with tribes grabbing at the best land available. More commonly, whole peoples were on the march as a result of the disruption caused by the Hun invasion.

# THE MOUNTED MILITARY CLASS

THE ASSOCIATION BETWEEN POSSESSION of horses and social status, and the choice to serve as mounted troops, has been a factor in European politics and military affairs since at least Roman times. The second echelon of Roman society, below the senators, were the Equites, who provided an integral cavalry element to the early legions.

In later eras of the empire, cavalry were recruited from barbarian peoples or raised as professional elements of the army. However, the expense of maintaining a horse and a full set of military equipment meant that, after the fall of the empire, mounted military service became the province of the wealthy and ultimately an expression of that wealth.

Although by the AD 450s the Huns were defeated, they had caused enormous turmoil in the lands they attacked. Tribes seeking to escape them, or directly displaced by them, moved westwards, which brought them into collision with their neighbours. These people, in turn, were pushed west, causing further displacement.

Thus began an era of mass migration known as the Volkswanderung, or Migration Era. Tribes fought each other and the remnants of the Roman Empire for land to settle on, while the remaining Roman forces were rallied in an increasingly vain attempt to secure parts of the empire. The Eastern Roman Empire went its own way, leaving its western cousins to fend for themselves.

The Volkswanderung began in a small way, with minor groups pushing west, but by the late 400s huge populations were on the march. These people all had to be fed, with food being obtained from the lands they passed through – which were already supporting a population. Conflict was inevitable and destruction with it. A migration that was successfully resisted might cause more long-term damage than one that was not, since a stalled march left tens of thousands of people in temporary camps foraging an area to the last scraps rather than passing through and moving on.

The Migration Era did not greatly affect Scandinavia, which was at the time developing its own culture. Scandinavia had some contact with the Roman world by way of trade and the occasional treaty, but it was not dependent on the vast Roman economy. Since the lands of the north were out of the path of the Hun incursions and the general push was westwards,

BELOW: The Pyrenees were a formidable obstacle to the migrating tribes. A scouting party or warband might cross the mountains with relatively little difficulty, but moving families and possessions was a different matter altogether.

Scandinavia continued on a path that **would** ultimately result in the arrival of the Norsemen, **or** Vikings, on the European stage.

In the meantime, the Migration Era saw Germanic people settling in the far west and Slavic groups moving into the newly vacated east of Europe. Just as there was no clear-cut beginning to these vast migrations, there was no one date when it all ended. However, by AD 700 the face of Europe had been completely changed. New states were emerging, based upon the culture of the tribes that had settled with an admixture of Roman ideas and values.

There was destruction and conflict, of course, and some of it was deliberate. However, there was no intentional destruction of Roman civilization by hordes of barbarians. Instead, the light of Rome was dimmed from within and smothered under the weight of a changing world. The last emperors in Rome were largely figureheads for the real rulers of western Europe, the leaders of what Romans still called 'barbarian' tribes.

In AD 474 Julius Nepos, an official from the Eastern Roman Empire sent to administrate the western territories, installed himself as emperor. He was deposed a year later by his general, Orestes, who had in his youth served Attila. Orestes then named his son Romulus Augustulus as emperor without approval from the Eastern Roman Empire.

Romulus Augustulus's reign was short. In AD 476 a dispute with the Germanic Heruli people led to conflict and Orestes's army mutinied in favour of Odoaster, another 'barbarian' holding high rank in the Roman Army. Romulus Augustulus was deposed, but Odoaster did not take the title of emperor. Instead, he styled himself as king, signalling the end of the Western Roman emperors.

The year AD 476 is widely taken as the date on which the Western Roman Empire ceased to exist. In reality, some areas continued to consider themselves 'Roman' and to use the imperial form of governance. Overall, though, Italy and all of western Europe was now ruled by people the Romans would have called barbarians. Young, brawling, energetic new states began to emerge, bringing about the Early Middle Ages.

ABOVE: **Julius Nepos** was the last emperor in the west to have official sanction. His successor took the office by force and was himself ousted the same way. The new 'barbarian' rulers of Rome soon did away with the pretence of being Romans altogether.

ЄΛЄΝΗ ΚΑΙ ΚѠΝC- ΤΑΝΤΙΝΟC

2

# THE BARBARIAN KINGDOMS

As the displaced tribes of Europe began to settle in their new lands, their traditional cultures melded with those of peoples they encountered on their journeys or conquered to gain a homeland. These new tribal cultures were the beginnings of the European kingdoms of the Middle Ages.

T HE WORD 'BARBARIAN' has connotations of backwardness and a propensity for mindless destruction or wanton violence, but this was not its original meaning. The word may have originated with the people of ancient Greece, who said that the language of those outside their culture consisted entirely of bar-bar-bar noises. Despite this rather condescending attitude, the ancient Greeks were willing to deal fairly and honourably with these 'barbarian' peoples and sometimes used a different word for them – Keltoi.

The people we refer to as Celts in modern times did not call themselves that. The Greeks used the term collectively for the 'barbarian' people of northern and western Europe, who probably referred to themselves by tribal, clan or family

OPPOSITE: **Emperor Justinian I and his wife Theodora managed to regain control over some western and north African provinces for a time. Ultimately, maintaining a hold on Rome proved beyond the resources of the Byzantine Empire.**

identity rather than some vague notion of an over-arching racial or cultural identity. These Keltoi did not build magnificent cities to rival those of ancient Greece, but they constructed organized towns and settlements, and possessed a complex and rich culture. Their metalworking skills were highly advanced, enabling the production of fine jewellery and resilient sword blades. The Keltoi to the north of Greece sometimes served as mercenaries in the wars of the Greek city states and at other times fought against them. Trading relations were in general good, enabling the Keltoi to import materials necessary to bronze-working.

THE ARMIES OF ROME LEARNED LESSONS FROM THE CELTIC PEOPLE AND EVEN GOT THEIR SWORDS FROM THEM, BUT ULTIMATELY THE GAULS OF MAINLAND EUROPE WERE SUBJUGATED.

The Bronze Age Collapse, beginning around 1200 BC, led to an interruption in trade with the Greeks and may have been a factor in the move to using iron. At that time, better tools could be made from bronze than iron due to the maturity of the techniques involved. Necessity forced innovation and, by the time the Greek Dark Age was over, the Keltoi were producing extremely good iron weapons and tools.

The Celtic people spread all across Europe, mingling with local cultures to create societies that blurred the boundaries of what was 'Celtic' and what was not. The Romans referred to the

RIGHT: Leaf-shaped blades were a characteristic of Celtic swords in many regions. These bronze examples were found in Ireland.

LEFT: The offer of tribute to save Rome from the conquering Gauls in 390 BC resulted in a dispute about weights and measures. Gaulish chief Brennus reputedly placed his sword upon the scales, suggesting that it would be unwise to quibble with the conquerors.

Celtic people of what is now France and the surrounding area as Gauls and applied the term to Celtic people in general.

Although not as organized as the Romans, the tribes of the Celts were powerful. Rome itself was sacked by an army of Gauls under the command of Brennus in 390 BC, and when Rome moved into the Iberian peninsula its leaders were so impressed with the sword-making skills of the people there – Celtiberians, as they are often called – that a version of their distinctive weapon was issued to the Roman legions.

The armies of Rome learned lessons from the Celtic people and even got their swords from them, but ultimately the Gauls of mainland Europe were subjugated. This was largely due to superior organization and logistical capability, plus the fact

ABOVE: The 'Roman'
short iron sword was
in fact invented by the
Celtiberians and adopted
after Roman troops
encountered it in battle.
It was replaced by longer
swords in the latter years
of the Roman Empire.

that Rome was united and the tribes usually were not. As a result, the Celtic people of Iberia, Gaul and the regions close to Italy became Romanized. They never completely lost their own identity, however.

Thus, when the displaced tribes arrived from the east it was not merely a Roman culture they overlaid with their own; it was also the remaining vestiges of the ancient Celtic people Rome had conquered. These were the influences that would shape the emerging states of Europe in AD 500.

## THE FRANKS

The Franks were a Germanic people who moved west from the region around the Rhine and Weser rivers. They were a tribal confederation rather than a single culture and it is not clear what they collectively called themselves, if they had a name for their grouping at all. It seems likely that each member group retained its tribal identity during the march westwards and the process of coalescing into a single culture began after resettlement in what is now France and Belgium.

There are numerous theories as to how the Franks gained the name we now know them by. It is possible that the origin was the francisca, a throwing axe favoured by at least some of the member tribes. If so, the name 'Franks' was imposed by Roman observers on the people who used these axes in battle. The term first appears in Roman writings around AD 257. Roman sources of this time name the Franks as wild and ferocious warriors who not only raided the inland cities of the empire but who were also adept mariners who attacked towns in the British Isles or pirated vessels in the coastal waters of the English Channel.

As the Roman Empire declined, it was more effective to recruit the Franks than to fight them. By this time the legions were increasingly 'barbarized', with non-Roman troops fighting in the manner of their parent cultures rather than being retrained as legionaries. The Frankish warrior of the period fought on foot, using a short spear called an angon as his weapon of choice. The angon could be thrown or used in hand-to-hand combat, as could the francisca. A heavy axe wielded in one hand, the francisca made a lethal short-range throwing implement that could split a shield or ricochet about among close-order enemies, possibly injuring more than one opponent.

The angon and francisca were backed up by a sword and dagger for close combat, leading to a typically Frankish tactic of hurling a volley of spears and axes and then charging home into the disorganized and dismayed enemy. This was not very different to the classical Roman pilum and gladius style of warfare, although the Franks never achieved Roman levels of logistical support or military organization.

ABOVE: The Battle of Tolbiac is usually dated to AD 496 but this is not certain. It is known that Clovis led the Franks to victory over the Alemanni, and that he converted to Christianity afterwards.

# THE LAST LEGIONS

IN THE LAST DAYS of the Roman Empire, its forces were still called legions but they were very different to the highly organized units of the past. Formations were much smaller and more lightly equipped. Legionary troops ceased to be exclusively heavy infantry and fought with spears and bows as well as the traditional sword and javelin. A few items of traditional legionary equipment remained in use, often in vestigial form, but the legions that failed to defend the remnants of the empire would not have been recognizable to those who fought to create it.

The Franks moved west into Belgium and eventually northern Gaul, supplying large numbers of warriors to the declining Roman Empire as members of its army and as allies fighting under their own banner. Franks would eventually become the largest non-Roman component of the empire's forces and, in the meantime, they consolidated their hold over northern Gaul. This land was granted to the Franks by treaty with Rome, although this agreement represented bowing to the inevitable to a great

RIGHT: The clothing worn by fourth-century Franks, and their general appearance, was more 'barbarian' than 'post-Roman'. Over time, dress and mannerisms evolved into those of an early medieval kingdom.

extent – the Roman Empire could not have stopped the barbarian invaders from taking the territory, so they made a virtue of necessity and negotiated a deal. The arrangement proved beneficial several times over; Frankish forces came to the aid of Rome and its Visigoth allies in AD 451 against Attila's Huns and fought against the Visigoths on the Roman side in AD 463.

## CLOVIS I

By the time of Clovis I (AD 466–511), the Franks were considered a kingdom rather than a tribal grouping. Clovis's descendants were known as the Merovingian dynasty after his grandfather Merovech, who fought against the Huns alongside Roman

ABOVE: **Clovis I wore purple – the colour of rulership in the Roman Empire – with the blessing of the Byzantine emperor. Connections with Rome still held great significance and conveyed an air of legitimacy upon the new lords of Europe.**

forces. The Merovingians were one of the earliest hereditary ruling houses of western Europe and arguably the architects of the nation of France. Clovis broke the last vestiges of Roman control over northern Gaul in a campaign against Syagrius, the last governor of Gaul. Syagrius's forces were defeated at Soissons in AD 486, making Clovis undisputed ruler of the region.

Syagrius notably did not flee to a Roman province but went to Toulouse, the capital of the Visigothic kingdom, where he presumably hoped to find refuge. It was not to be; Alaric II of the Visigoths chose not to harbour an enemy of the powerful Franks and surrendered him to Clovis, who is generally thought to have beheaded his enemy.

Mercy towards defeated enemies or potential rivals was not a luxury a barbarian king could afford and the actions of Clovis were repeated many times throughout the Middle Ages; innocent royal relatives were executed for no more pressing reason than the possibility that one day someone might rise in rebellion in their name – whether they wanted any part of it or not.

ABOVE: Syagrius ruled an enclave of territory that still considered itself to be Roman. His defeat by Clovis I at the Battle of Soissons removed the last vestige of the Roman Empire west of Italy.

So it was with Clovis I. His cousins and potential rivals, Chararic and Ragnachar, had sent forces to assist in the war against Syagrius, although Chararic's army hung back during the decisive battle. Believing Chararic to be hedging his bets, Clovis captured him and initially forced both Chararic and his heir to become priests. Careless words convinced Clovis that they were plotting to rebel against him, so he had them both put to death and annexed their lands.

Although Ragnachar had actually fought alongside him at Soissons, Clovis deposed and executed him. By getting rid of his rivals and taking their lands, he succeeded in both increasing and securing his power. He also made war on the Visigoths, capturing several cities including Reims and Paris from them, and drove back incursions by the Alemanni when they tried to cross the Rhine into his territory.

Clovis had not inherited a rich or well-supplied kingdom, but his early successes in battle inspired his followers to stay with him and he was able to reward them from the spoils of war. Here again can be seen the beginnings of the politico-military system of the Middle Ages, with a charismatic king directly leading his warriors and service translating directly to wealth and social status.

Clovis began his career as a pagan and, although converting to Christianity offered political advantages, he seemed set against it even after marrying Clotilde, a Burgundian Christian. However, he saw the 'hand of God' in his victories over the Alemanni and the recovery of his children from illness and enthusiastically embraced the new religion. This was a factor in renewed war against the Visigoths, which further increased the territory of the Franks.

Clovis might not have been so successful against the Visigoths if he had not embraced Christianity. The Byzantine emperor, Anastasius, was a Nicaean Christian but Theodosius, king of the Ostrogoths in Italy, was an Arian Christian. Theodosius owed allegiance to the emperor, who had supported his rise to power, and obeyed his injunction against aiding Alaric II of the Visigoths – who was a fellow Arian – against the newly Nicaean Clovis.

The marriage of Theodosius to Clovis's sister Audofleda was another factor. Theodosius had wanted this union as part of

BELOW: A depiction of war between the Franks and Visigoths, showing mounted combat with couched lances. This is unlikely to be accurate; the armoured horseman would not come to dominate warfare for many years.

# ARIAN VS NICAEAN CHRISTIANITY

In the early fourth century AD, a Christian priest named Arius set forth a belief that rather than all three parts of the Holy Trinity being a single God, Jesus was created by God and therefore dependent on him for his existence. This belief was denounced as heresy by the Council of Nicaea, causing a major schism in the early Christian Church.

The result was ongoing conflict and sometimes persecution between followers of the two sects, which at times expanded into major wars between the emerging states of Europe.

an alliance with the Franks, but he had also married his own daughter to Alaric in a similar gambit. With dynastic alliance commitments more or less deadlocked, it was the influence of the Byzantine emperor, who would not countenance an alliance of Arians against a Nicaean, that decided Theodosius's stance on the conflict. He did manage to annex some territory at the expense of Clovis's ambitions, however.

THE PASSING OF A METAPHORICAL TORCH DOWN FROM THE ANCIENT AND IDEALIZED CIVILIZATION OF ROME CAN STILL BE DISCERNED IN SOME CEREMONIES.

The Visigoths were defeated and Alaric II was killed. They retired into the Iberian peninsula, leaving Clovis's Franks in almost complete control of what would become – not coincidentally – France. The Byzantine emperor presented Clovis with a purple tunic, the mark of a Roman consul. The trappings of the Roman Empire still held a certain mystique and rulers in many cases saw themselves – or tried to present themselves – as the rightful successors to the Romans. This connection never entirely faded; even in modern times, the passing of a metaphorical torch down from the ancient and idealized civilization of Rome can still be discerned in some ceremonies and symbology.

Clovis made his capital at Paris and, although he did lose some territory to the Ostrogoths, he left behind a stable and powerful kingdom after his death. This is normally dated as AD 511 but a case can be made for 513. Clovis divided his kingdom

between his four sons rather than naming one as sole ruler, ending the brief unity of the Franks and setting the stage for power plays and infighting that prevented further expansion.

## THE FRANKS AFTER CLOVIS

The division of the Frankish kingdom might have been disastrous, but the successors of Clovis were willing and able to limit their conflicts, establishing what might be considered rudimentary 'rules of war' that were mostly followed. Enormous economic damage was generally avoided, but the power plays of the Frankish noble families absorbed much of

ABOVE: This fifteenth-century depiction of the Battle of Vouille has both sides equipped in the manner of the time – a common error in medieval art. The warriors of 507 would not have possessed such advanced armour.

PREMIÈRE RACE
dite Mérovingienne

| Clovis II. | Bathilde | Clotaire III. | Childéric II. | Thierry I. | Clovis III. |
|---|---|---|---|---|---|
| 638 — 655. | | 655 — 670. | 670 — 673. | 673 — 691. | 691 — 695. |

ABOVE: **Merovingian kings and queens: Clovis II and Balthild, Chlothar III, Childeric II, Theuderic III and Clovis III. During their reign actual power shifted to the mayors of the palace.**

OPPOSITE: **Queen Brunhilda of Austrasia was torn apart by horses, an incident that appears (in various forms with different participants) in a number of European legends and folk tales.**

their attention and made unified action against outsiders an impossibility. There were exceptions to this norm, with some feuds vindictively prosecuted beyond territorial or political gain, but over time the kingdom of the Franks became four relatively powerful states that would be highly influential throughout the Middle Ages.

Of these states, Aquitaine lay on the Atlantic coast north of the Pyrenees, Burgundy southeast of Paris and Neustria to the north of Paris. The original homeland of the Franks in northeast France and across the Rhine constituted Austrasia. Conflict between these states was near-constant, with some or even all of them occasionally united under a single ruler. This was achieved by Chlothar II, king of Neustria, who defeated Queen Brunhilda of Austrasia in AD 613 after a long and bitter conflict. After putting Brunhilda to death by having her pulled apart by teams of horses, Chlothar annexed the lands of his other rivals less violently.

Although Chlothar II succeeded in making himself king of all Franks, at least for a time, his reign actually saw the power of the crown diminished and that of the senior nobility increased. This ultimately led to the downfall of the Merovingian dynasty. By the mid-700s AD, power had shifted sufficiently that the last Merovingian king, Childeric III, was little more than a figurehead. He was deposed by the Mayor of the Palace, Pippin (or Pepin) III, known as 'The Short', in AD 751. The deposition was relatively merciful; Childeric was sent off to a monastery while Pippin the Short became the first of the Carolingian rulers of France.

BELOW: A seventeenth-century engraving of Charles Martel, arguably one of the most influential figures in European history. His victory at Tours permitted the Christian Church to remain dominant in Europe.

## CHARLES MARTEL: 'THE HAMMER'

The last years of the Merovingian dynasty were not lacking in glory. Charles Martel, nicknamed 'The Hammer', successfully defended Europe from Muslim forces moving up from Spain in one of the great turning points of history. His career did not begin auspiciously; the young Charles was imprisoned during a dispute over succession rights. The intent was to prevent him becoming a rallying point for challenges against the crown, but in AD 715 he escaped and began to do what his enemies had feared.

By AD 718, Charles Martel had secured his position as the foremost power in Francia and subsequently conducted campaigns in Bavaria and Alemannia. However, Muslim forces were advancing into Francia from the Iberian peninsula despite vigorous resistance and a new approach to warfare was required to counter them.

Recognizing that a trained army was necessary to counter the disciplined Muslim forces, Charles Martel began gathering funds to create one. This was accomplished at the expense of Church property; lands were seized despite the objections of religious officials and the funds this raised were spent on the army. As a result, the force Charles Martel led to confront the invaders was steady and professional. Occupying a good defensive position near Tours, the Franks were able to repel repeated cavalry charges that would have broken a less experienced force.

The Battle of Tours (sometimes referred to as the Battle of Poitiers) turned back the Muslim invasion of Europe but was not the end of the conflict. Successfully integrating heavy cavalry into his army, Charles Martel defeated the invaders again and brought the threat of conquest to an end. He died in AD 741, dividing his lands between his sons Carloman and Pippin III, who would instigate the replacement of the Merovingian dynasty with his son's Carolingian line.

THE FRANKISH INFANTRYMAN WITH HIS AXE WAS SUPPLANTED BY A MOUNTED WARRIOR WHO WOULD BECOME THE MAIN FORCE IN EUROPEAN WARFARE.

By the end of the Merovingian era, the France of the Middle Ages was beginning to take shape. The great realms that would feature prominently in medieval history now existed and, increasingly, the Frankish infantryman with his characteristic throwing axe was supplanted by a mounted warrior who would become the main force in European warfare for the next thousand years.

## THE VISIGOTHS

The Visigoths (or 'Western Goths') were described by Roman writers as a Germanic people, although it is unclear how long they had been dwelling in what the Romans called Germania, or even where. The term 'Visigoth' was later applied by Roman writers to differentiate the Western and Eastern Goths, though not all Roman historians were so picky. Indeed, the Goths are first recorded in Roman writings as a 'Scythian' tribe.

The term 'Scythian' generally has connotations of horse-using peoples, but it appears to have been used rather vaguely to describe any tribal group living in the vicinity of the Black Sea. The Goths do not appear to have been related to the Scythian people of the steppes and even this supposed homeland is open to some doubt.

# THE BATTLE OF TOURS

Estimates of the forces involved in the battle of Tours vary wildly. What is certain is that the forces of the Umayyad Caliphate had penetrated deep into Europe and seemed capable of defeating any opposition sent against them. The primary striking force of this army was lightly armoured cavalry capable of skirmishing or making a massed charge. Led with aggression and initiative, Muslim cavalry was capable of outflanking and overrunning the ill-disciplined forces of its enemies.

By the time the Muslim force reached Tours, it was burdened by a vast quantity of plunder and had suffered attrition along the way from combat and the inevitable friction of war. Nevertheless, this was a powerful force requiring a careful response. What set Charles Martel apart from other rulers of his time was a grasp of organization and the importance of logistics. Rather than raise whatever troops he could to augment his small bodyguard, he created a force of professional infantry, supplying them with good armour and weapons. More importantly, this was a standing force that could train year-round, and by the time it met the invaders its personnel were confident in both their own fighting power and the reliability of their fellows.

The Muslim force was rather complacent by this point and did not act to prevent the Franks from setting up a good defensive position where cavalry would have to attack them uphill. As a result, the battle was preceded by a six-day standoff during which the Muslim leader, Emir Abd-ar-Rahman, considered his options. The Franks were better equipped for the cold weather and Abd-ar-Rahman eventually faced a decision to attack or give up the campaign. His force launched a series of cavalry charges that at times penetrated the defensive square formation of the Franks. This might have broken a less well-trained force, but the Franks retained reserves within the square and those on the outer faces had the confidence to fight on while their intruders were dealt with behind them.

Meanwhile, a detached force of Franks managed to get into the Muslim camp where they freed prisoners and caused a great deal of confusion. This distraction – and fears the Franks were about to make off with all their plunder – pulled warriors back from the attack on the main Frankish force. Rahman himself was killed trying to rally his troops, leaving no clear successor for command. The Franks were unable to pursue cavalrymen on foot, so reformed their defensive position and waited.

The Franks at Tours were in a position where they had to merely avoid defeat in order to achieve their strategic aims, whereas the Muslim force had to win the battle to continue the campaign. Having been resoundingly repulsed, losing their commander in the process, they chose to retire to Iberia with their loot. The defensive victory at Tours prevented Muslim victory but Charles Martel was not able to follow up or take the initiative; not with an infantry army against highly mobile cavalry. Thus the wars continued, with further incursions into Francia at intervals. Much as the Roman Army found it needed cavalry to deal with the Huns and similar mounted opponents, the Franks began fielding their own cavalry in later years, ultimately leading to the rise of European chivalry.

BELOW: A rather fanciful depiction of the Battle of Tours. The actual battle was a victory for the Franks' defensive tactics over the aggressive cavalry of the Muslim Army.

ABOVE: Mounted archers such as those used by the Scythians performed the remarkable feat of shooting in any direction while riding at speed – without stirrups.

The Goths may have originally come from Scandinavia or the region north of the Black Sea, although there is much debate about this. The earliest Roman scholars to write about them knew little for sure and, in some cases, have proven to be unreliable on other matters. Likewise, there is archaeological evidence of Gothic tombs near Gdansk in Poland, but it is debatable whether this was their homeland or an area they occupied for a time during a larger migration.

By the end of the first century AD, the Goths were better known to the Romans. Tacitus wrote about them in his work *Germania* and describes characteristics thoroughly associated with the Germanic tribes: red hair, a tendency to be large and of robust build, and ferocious in combat. Although apparently preferring to fight on foot, the Goths are described as possessing skilful cavalry who could carry out battlefield evolutions as a disciplined body.

Armour was rare among these early Goths. They are
described as sometimes being 'naked' but this does not
necessarily mean they wore nothing at all. Nakedness has been
used to imply going shirtless – bare-chested but certainly not
entirely naked – or lacking in armour protection. Although a
number of artworks depict entirely naked barbarians, often
committing acts of violence or destruction, this seems rather
fanciful. Apart from anything else, the north European climate
is not really conducive to a lack of clothing, and warriors
lacking the protection of footwear and trousers would be

LEFT: An image of the
Visigoth invasion of Iberia,
depicting the tribesmen as
wild and savage. In reality
the Goths were no more
'barbaric' than any other
people of the time.

severely impaired by thorny undergrowth of a sort found in profusion in their homelands.

The typical early Goth warrior was armed only with a spear and shield. The latter was richly decorated, whereas most of their war gear is described as being plain in appearance. Bows, javelins, swords and daggers were also used, though without any uniformity. Warriors fought with what they had and organization was along charismatic lines. Leaders were expected to outdo their followers in courage; followers were expected to match their leader's valour. The result was a ferocious and vigorous way of making war, but one that could lead to disaster against a more disciplined opponent.

RIGHT: Division of the Roman Empire between four rulers was intended to improve governance, but ultimately caused more conflict. Licinius managed to defeat the usurper Maximinus but was in turn defeated by Constantine at Adrianople in AD 323.

By the late third century AD, the Visigoths were apparently using that name for themselves, although it had been coined by Roman writers. They had absorbed newcomers from other tribes, some of them displaced by the increasingly threatening Huns, and were themselves feeling the pressure. The Visigoths moved south into the Danube region and sought permission from the Roman authorities to settle there as foederati.

## GOTHIC WARS

Mistreatment by Roman officials led to the Gothic Wars, during which they defeated and killed Emperor Valens at the Battle of Adrianople. The conflict was resolved with treaties that granted lands to the Visigoths and they became increasingly Christianized during this period. The Visigoth king Alaric I attempted to implement a number of Roman customs and institutions among his people, which met with moderate success. Had events taken a different turn, the Visigoths might have infused the region with a new Romano-Gothic vigour and could even have ushered in a new era of the empire. However, Rome clung to its one-sided treaties with the Visigoths and, in an effort to force a renegotiation, Alaric made war upon the Western Roman Empire.

In AD 410, Alaric's Visigoths captured Rome. Even sacking the city could not convince the emperor to make a new and fairer treaty, so Alaric resolved to push on. His intention was to go to North Africa via Sicily, but after his death his successor Athaulf chose southern Gaul as his destination. Athaulf and his successors carved out a kingdom based around Toulouse and gradually expanded it until the Visigoths controlled a significant part of the Iberian peninsula as well.

ABOVE: Emperor Valens faced a challenge from Procopius, who bought the loyalty of nearby legions and used them to take control of Thrace. Valens was initially inclined to negotiate but decided to fight instead. Procopius' troops deserted him, leading to his capture and execution.

ABOVE: A late nineteenth-century depiction of the Visigoths sacking Rome. The image of naked barbarians tearing down the great works of civilization has endured in the popular imagination long after it should have been dispelled.

Conflict with the Franks of northern Gaul was perhaps inevitable but was exacerbated by differences within the Christian Church. The Visigoths had embraced Arian Christianity; the Franks adopted Nicaean ways. It is possible that a clash occurred as early as AD 502, and in 507 full-scale war broke out. It is widely surmised that Clovis I of the Franks was fighting a religious war against his Arian neighbours, but the goal may have been simple territorial conquest.

The conflict reached a climax with a battle near Poitiers, normally known as the Battle of Vouille. Contemporary accounts are conflicting and often biased, some suggesting the Franks were assisted by Burgundian forces and others omitting any mention of them. Alaric's army contained a mix of Visigothic warriors and troops trained and equipped in the Roman fashion, who were outfought by their Frankish opponents. Although Clovis narrowly escaped death at one point, it was Alaric who was killed. His army fled, opening the way for the Franks to advance on Toulouse.

With their king dead and their capital plundered, the Visigoths retreated into Iberia, where they made their capital at Toledo. Over the next two centuries, the lines blurred between the Romano-Iberian natives and the Visigoths until they became a single culture. The Muslim invasion of Iberia in the early 700s AD was vigorously, though unsuccessfully, resisted by the Visigoths. After the defeat of the Muslim army at Tours by an army of Franks under the command of Charles Martel, conflict

# TROJAN ORIGINS?

Some sources claim that the Goths were descended from the people of Troy, but this is extremely unlikely. It is more probable that the connection was invented to give the upstart barbarian rulers of the former Roman Empire a noble heritage. They were not the only culture to claim descent from ancient Troy.

It is said that Rome was founded by Trojans fleeing the destruction of their home city and that a man of Roman or Trojan descent discovered Britain. From him came the line of legendary rulers that included King Arthur and the leaders of various tribes among the Britons. Even the Norse gods were claimed to reside in Troy by some sources, commuting to Asgard every day by way of the magical Bifröst bridge.

Some of these tales are obviously invention, whereas others might have a kernel of truth. Little is known about Troy other than what is recorded in Homer's *Iliad* and *Odyssey*, and these are derived from oral histories (or possibly invented stories) passed down through the Greek Dark Age. Archaeology has proven that a great city once stood where Troy is said to have been, but beyond that little is known for sure. Even in antiquity, Troy was a legendary place and a natural choice when inventing descent from noble ancestors to legitimize power.

BELOW: Aeneas and his son are credited – in some stories at least – with founding Rome. This gave Romans a link back to the legendary city of Troy.

in Iberia continued. The former Visigoths emerged from these struggles as the foundation of the Spanish kingdoms.

## THE OSTROGOTHS

The term 'Ostrogoth' appears to be a misinterpretation of the tribe's own name for itself, taken to mean 'Eastern Goth' by Roman historians. Sharing a common ancestry and origin with the Visigoths, the Ostrogoths lived in the region around the Black Sea and proved at times to be troublesome neighbours for Roman provinces in the area.

By the time of the Hun invasion, the Ostrogoths ruled a large area but were unable to avoid subjugation. While the Visigoths moved west into the Roman Empire, the Ostrogoths were overrun. Their king, Ermanaric, is said to have committed suicide when it became obvious he could not defend his people against the Huns.

Ostrogoth warriors fought in the wars of the Huns as they expanded eastwards, until after the death of Attila they were able to free themselves. Under the leadership of Theodoric, the Ostrogoths invaded Italy – with Byzantine approval – in AD 474. Odoacer, a Germanic leader, had deposed Romulus Augustulus and thereby ended the line of Western Roman emperors. Defeating him, Theodoric realigned Rome with Byzantium.

RIGHT: The Battle of the Catalaunian Fields saw Attila's Huns finally turned back from their conquest of Europe. Much of the cost of victory fell upon the Franks, who lost their king along with many of his warriors.

The Ostrogothic kingdom in
Italy was established AD 493 and
represented a melding of Roman
and Germanic ideas. Roman art
and social customs were preserved
and, although the Ostrogothic
kingdom was separate from the
Byzantine Empire, relations were
good until AD 534. Amalasvintha,
daughter of Theodoric, assumed
the throne after a period as regent
to her son but was killed in a
palace power struggle. Her cousin
Theodahad took the throne,
triggering an intervention by the
Byzantine Empire.

The empire sent Flavius
Belisarius, its great general, to
remove Theodahad from power.
After repeated defeats, the
Ostrogoths themselves deposed Theodahad but his successor was
equally overmatched. A combination of warfare, internal plotting
and negotiation resulted in Belisarius taking control of the whole
Ostrogothic kingdom in the name of Emperor Justinian.

Justinian was concerned that his general might be growing
too powerful, so Belisarius was recalled to Byzantium and other
officials were sent to govern Italy. This was not to the liking of
the Ostrogoths, who rose up against their new overlords. Led
by Baduila, who is better known as Totila, the Ostrogoths were
successful for a while. Baduila was killed in battle in AD 552
and within a year the rising had been crushed. After this, the
Ostrogoths gradually lost their identity as such, becoming part of
a mixed southern European culture.

ABOVE: **A sixth-century
mosaic depicting
Byzantine emperor
Justinian with his
attendants. Justinian
managed to reclaim
some of the Western
provinces for a time, and
broke the power of the
Vandal kingdom.**

## THE VANDALS

As with other tribal peoples of the era, the origin of the Vandals
is unclear. They may have migrated south out of Scandinavia and

there is evidence of their presence in Poland. The name Vandal is thought to have originated with Roman writers, who also called them the Lugi. It is not clear how unified the Vandals were as a people, but it is known that the Hasdingi Vandals moved into the Roman Empire as foederati in the late second century AD. Their cousins, the Silingi, settled in what is now Silesia.

Relations between Rome and its barbarian foederati were often troubled and the Vandals were no exception. At times, they gave good service; on other occasions, they were the enemy. The Vandals embraced Arian Christianity, which put them at odds with the Nicaean Romans. This may have been a factor in the decision not to permit the Vandals to move into the empire as pressure from the Huns increased. Instead, the Vandals took advantage of reduced Roman strength along the Rhine and in AD 406 forced their way into the empire.

THE PLUNDERING OF ROME IN AD 445 WAS INTOLERABLE TO THE BYZANTINE EMPEROR, WHO SAW THE VANDALS AS A THREAT TO THE MEDITERRANEAN REGION.

The Vandals faced fierce competition from other Germanic tribes seeking a safe homeland and did not settle in Gaul. Instead, they pushed through into Iberia where they set up a kingdom under Gunderic, who also ruled the Alans. The Vandals built a navy to operate on the Mediterranean, which ultimately gave them the ability to move into North Africa. In the meantime, they fought against other tribes for control of Iberia, notably the Visigoths.

### GAISERIC

Gunderic died in AD 428, to be succeeded by Gaiseric. At the same time, plotting within the Roman world created an opportunity for the new Vandal king. According to some sources, Boniface, governor in North Africa, was falsely accused of treason by his rival, Flavius Aetius. As the situation escalated towards war, Boniface asked the Vandals to assist him. Other sources have the Vandals as instigators of an invasion of North Africa for reasons of their own.

Whatever the truth of it, Gaiseric landed a large number of Vandals in North Africa. The figure of 80,000 is agreed by some sources but remains open to debate. Gaiseric's force was certainly large; it proved sufficient to capture Carthage and the surrounding cities, giving Gaiseric control of Rome's most important grain-producing provinces.

War with Carthage had long ago necessitated creating a Roman Navy and now a new maritime threat was based out of the same harbour. Gaiseric already possessed a large naval force; controlling Carthage allowed it to raid coastal areas all around the Mediterranean, as well as preying on merchant traffic. Roman attempts to reconquer the lost provinces came to naught and in AD 442 a treaty was agreed recognizing Gaiseric as ruler of the Vandal North African kingdom.

By AD 445, the political situation had changed. The Roman Emperor Valentinian III was killed by Petronius Maximus, giving Gaiseric an excuse to declare his treaty with Rome void. Gaiseric's argument was that the treaty was an agreement between himself and Valentinian – without whom there was no deal. Whatever Rome thought of this interpretation was irrelevant – Gaiseric launched an invasion of Italy and there was no force sufficient to stop him.

Gaiseric landed at Ostia, Rome's port, and advanced on the city. A siege could have only one ending but would cause immense harm to both sides, so the Vandals were invited to plunder the city so long as they caused as little destruction as possible. Gaiseric honoured this deal but, despite the fact that the sacking of Rome by the Vandals was vastly milder than what usually happened when a city was taken, his people's name still became a byword for wanton destruction.

BELOW: This stereotypical nineteenth-century image of bloodthirsty barbarians sweeping their foes before them could be almost any of the post-Roman peoples of Europe. In this case it is Vandals, advancing on Rome.

The plundering of Rome in AD 445 was intolerable to the Byzantine emperor, who now saw the Vandals as a threat to the whole Mediterranean region. Far from being the ignorant destroyer barbarian kings were often portrayed to be, Gaiseric understood the value of preparation and maintained a good intelligence network. Informed that a fleet was being assembled to send against him, he launched an attack and destroyed much of it.

In AD 468, Byzantium made another attempt to overthrow Vandal sea power, this time in conjunction with the Western Roman Empire. The Vandal fleet defeated the joint Roman force without undue difficulty, forcing the emperor to accept a treaty with Gaiseric. The Vandal kingdom dominated the Mediterranean until Gaiseric's death in AD 478.

## THE VANDALS AFTER GAISERIC

Vandal power peaked under Gaiseric and declined quickly under his successors. Internal disputes, some of them religious in nature, weakened the kingdom and distracted the Vandals from their external ambitions. Finally, the persecution of Nicaean Christians by the Arian Vandals prompted Emperor Justinian to launch an invasion of North Africa.

RIGHT: The capture and plundering of Rome in AD 445 marked the high point of Vandal power. As with many charismatic leaders, Gaiseric was not followed by equally talented men, and his kingdom declined thereafter.

# CHARISMATIC LEADERSHIP

The combination of charisma and ability in certain individuals – Clovis, Attila, Gaiseric, Charles Martel and others – had an overwhelming impact on the development of early Europe. Often these men caused profound changes in their lifetimes, only for their work to be undone by the mistakes of less talented successors. This pattern would be repeated throughout the early medieval period, with the fortunes of a culture or country rising and falling depending on the ability of their rulers. Nowhere was this more apparent than in battle, where the sight of a king fleeing or being felled could break an army that was otherwise quite capable of winning the day.

The Vandal king, Gelimer, was no Gaiseric. He only learned of the Byzantine force as it approached Carthage overland. Quickly formulating a plan to pincer and destroy the Byzantine force, Gelimer marched to meet them in what would become known as the Battle of Ad Decimum. Gelimer's battle plan was over-complex and relied on precise timing, which was simply not possible. As a result – instead of halting the Byzantine advance – the first Vandal force to engage was roughly handled, leaving the way to Carthage open. The second column was driven off by Hun cavalry in Byzantine service.

The main Vandal force under Gelimer himself arrived where the rear of the Byzantine Army would have been if its march had been blocked, only to find the enemy had moved on. Gelimer pursued but found Carthage had been taken. He laid siege to his own capital, eventually forcing the outnumbered Byzantines to come out and fight. The Vandal Army, though more numerous, was dismayed by the ferocity of the Byzantine cavalry and, fearing the day lost, Gelimer fled the field. This led to a general rout.

Gelimer was captured in AD 534 and the power of the Vandal kingdom broken. Religious conflict continued and, with no

IN AD 468, BYZANTIUM MADE ANOTHER ATTEMPT TO OVERTHROW VANDAL SEA POWER, THIS TIME IN CONJUNCTION WITH THE WESTERN ROMAN EMPIRE.

BELOW: Poor strategic
and tactical decisions
cost Gelimer, king of
the Vandals, his capital.
His choice to flee the
battlefield caused a
collapse in his army
and ensured the defeat
became permanent.

coherent state emerging from the chaos, the remnants of the Vandals were unable to resist the attacks of the Moors. What remained of the Vandal people were dispersed or lost their cultural identity, and the great Vandal kingdom of North Africa faded from history.

## THE LOMBARDS

The Lombards were known to Roman historians from the first century AD although, as always, their accounts are based upon patchy or entirely incorrect information. The Lombards migrated into eastern Europe from Scandinavia, coming into conflict with other tribes along the way. They settled for a time in what is now Austria, later moving to the Danube region.

The Lombards appear to have been staunch Roman allies until the mid-500s AD. Lombard warriors fought alongside Eastern Roman troops against the Ostrogoths and allied with the Avars against the Gepids. Although that war was won, the agreement with the Avars benefited them far more than the Lombards, who were eclipsed by their former allies.

With no prospect of reversing the situation, the Lombard king Alboin led his people on a migration into Italy. The destruction of Totila's Ostrogothic forces there created opportunities, which were probably exploited by Alboin on his own initiative. It has been suggested that Roman officials invited the Lombards to settle in Italy, although this remains debatable.

From AD 568, the Lombards advanced into Italy, where they established a realm based on Verona. Most cities offered little resistance, although Pavia required a long siege. Once established, King Alboin divided up his new territory into duchies and allowed their rulers a great deal of autonomy. As a result, the Lombard realm became fragmented and prone to infighting and rivalries that distracted from external threats.

Alboin was assassinated in AD 572 at the instigation of his wife. The already divided Lombard realm fragmented further and might have entirely come apart had the Byzantine Empire not launched a bid to reclaim Italy as its territory. The threat of invasion prompted the Lombard dukes to elect a king to lead them, placing Authari on the throne in AD 584. Authari made his capital at Pavia and ruled until his death in AD 590. This period saw near-constant warfare against the Franks, the Byzantine Empire and rebels among his own people.

Authari's successor, Agilulf, was able to secure peace with the Franks and acted to consolidate his own power over the dukes. With the Byzantine Empire distracted by other conflicts, Agilulf strengthened his realm and apparently avoided the religious conflicts that had beset other kingdoms. Although Arian and Nicene Christians were at odds within the Lombard kingdom, there was comparatively little outright conflict or persecution.

ABOVE: After capturing Pavia, Alboin, king of the Lombards, established a system of duchies that foreshadowed the fragmented city-state politics of Italy in later centuries.

The Lombards gradually lost their tribal character and adopted many customs of the late Roman Empire. Their kingdom reached its peak around AD 640, controlling the north of Italy and parts of the south. However, the assassination of King Rodoald shortly after his father's death resulted in two Lombard realms, one centred on Pavia and one with its capital at Milan. Conflict continued for many years until the realm was reunited by Liutprand.

Liutprand's reign, from AD 712 to 744, saw a resurgence of Lombard power. Good relations with the powerful Franks permitted an expansion of the realm, but this was a short-lived heyday. After Liutprand's death, his successor Hildeprand was deposed by Ratchis, one of his dukes. Ratchis made the curious

decision to abdicate and retire to a monastery, but attempted to regain his throne in AD 756.

Ratchis's challenge was made against King Desiderius, who at the time had the support of the pope. Desiderius was successful in putting down other rebellions and sought to secure his position by a diplomatic marriage between his daughter and Charlemagne of the Franks. The marriage lasted only from AD 770 to 771, when Charlemagne sent her home and married again.

Charlemagne was at that time co-ruler of the Franks with his brother Carloman, an uneasy situation that Desiderius hoped to exploit. Desiderius's alliance with Carloman, intended to overthrow Charlemagne, came to nothing when Carloman died in AD 771. Desiderius came into conflict with Pope Adrian I, who refused to crown Carloman's sons or recognize their right to the Frankish kingdom. The result was war with the Franks and defeat at the hands of Charlemagne. Although Lombard dukes continued to rule in some areas, this was the end of the Lombard realm.

THEIR GOAL MAY HAVE BEEN TO ESTABLISH A SECURE HOMELAND FAR FROM THE GOKTURKS, ALTHOUGH THEIR EFFORTS INITIALLY LED TO MORE CONFLICT.

## THE AVARS

The Avars are mentioned in Roman sources as early as AD 463, when they appear to be associated with the Huns. However, it is entirely possible that this was a use of the same name for two different tribes or a misunderstanding on the part of Roman historians. Other sources state that the Avars migrated west from Mongolia after being defeated by the Gokturks there.

The Avars are recorded as being present on the steppes north of the Black Sea in the mid-550s AD and were used as mercenaries by the Byzantine Empire at times. They came to control a wide territory, eventually pushing into the Danube region and displacing the Lombards. Their goal may have been to establish a secure homeland far from the Gokturks, although their efforts initially led to more conflict. Barred from moving south of the Danube by Roman forces, the Avars tried to move west by a more northerly route but were repelled by the Franks.

OPPOSITE: Ermengarda (better known to history as Desiderata), daughter of King Desiderius, was sent home to her father after only one year of marriage to Charlemagne. War between the Lombards and Franks followed soon after.

ABOVE: **The Avars and other 'barbarian' people of the post-Roman world were capable of creating beautiful and intricate decorative items, which might be considered one of the hallmarks of civilization.**

Repeated attempts to take one or the other of these routes failed, until the Avars instead moved into Pannonia. They allied with the Lombards against the Gepids and benefited greatly from a one-sided deal they somehow persuaded the Lombards to accept. The king of the Lombards, Alboin, tried to cement an alliance with his former enemies by marrying Rosamund, the captured daughter of the Gepid chief. This would eventually be his undoing: Rosamund conspired to have him killed. It is said that Bayan, king of the Avars, made a wine cup from the skull of Rosamund's father and presented it to Alboin – who rather unwisely forced his new wife to drink from it.

In the meantime, the Lombards moved west into Italy, leaving the Avars in control of Pannonia. The capital at Sirmium fell to Bayan's forces in AD 582 and, with Byzantine forces distracted by campaigns in Persia, the Avars were able to ravage the Balkans for several years. They were heavily defeated in AD 602 but escaped total destruction when a combination of rebellion and plague crippled the Byzantine Empire's military forces.

Avar power was greatly diminished and their great leader Bayan appears to have died either before the defeats or from plague. He was succeeded by less effective leaders who nevertheless continued to make war on Byzantium. The Avars had started out as a nomadic horse people, but by AD 626 they were capable of fielding naval forces for an unsuccessful attack on Byzantium. Soon afterwards, their Bulgar subject people revolted, requiring a costly campaign to restore control. The decline continued, accelerated by internal conflicts, and in AD 795 the remnant of the Avars tried to align themselves with Charlemagne's Franks.

Charlemagne appears to have been receptive to this idea at first but ultimately conquered the Avars, who tried to assert their independence in a final revolt in AD 799. Once this was put down, the Avars became a subject people of the Franks.

## OTHER GERMANIC TRIBES

The tribes known to Roman scholars as 'Germanic' may or may not have all been culturally or genetically related, and the

## STIRRUPS

The introduction of the stirrup to Europe is hotly debated, but the Avars are widely credited. Stirrups allowed a rider to stand up to deliver a powerful downwards blow and, more importantly, to keep his seat if his horse stumbled or he over-extended on an attack. Stirrup-using horsemen were therefore more survivable on the battlefield than those who were more likely to be unseated; they could also lean further to reach an opponent while staying out of range of his weapon. The stirrup did not revolutionize warfare but it was a potent force multiplier for cavalry. The success of Avar horsemen and those who emulated them demonstrated this new technology in the most graphic manner possible and soon no self-respecting mounted warrior would be without his stirrups.

ABOVE: Like many great inventions, the stirrup is simple in concept but highly effective in use. Stirrups became a necessity for mounted warriors.

situation is complicated by the absorption of other peoples and cultural changes over time and during the migrations of various tribal groups. Designations such as Vandal or Goth are vague and were applied by outsiders at a particular time, so they may have included people of a quite different origin to the majority of the group. It is likely that the tribes defined themselves as having a local identity and affiliations or alliances with other tribes rather than being part of some over-arching Germanic, Gothic or Lombard nation.

Many tribes were part of the general 'Germanic' migrations without being major players or even considering themselves part of wider events. They were simply people looking for a home and trying to keep themselves fed. It is reasonable to suggest that tribes would find themselves swept up in events beyond their leaders' control, trying to make the most of opportunities and survive setbacks. Most of these tribes or tribal groups are little known to modern scholars, lost in the general upheaval of the early post-Roman period. Some, however, made their mark on history.

The Burgundians probably shared a common origin with many other Germanic tribes, perhaps in southern Scandinavia, and appear to have migrated south into what is now Poland along with other Germanic-to-be groups; Tacitus, writing in AD 98, mentions them there. The Burgundiones, as contemporary writers called them, were part of the Vandal migration across the Rhine. They met only weak opposition

BELOW: **The campaigns of Charlemagne – in this case against the Avars – marked the transition for the Franks from a post-Roman 'barbarian kingdom' into an early medieval realm.**

from Romanized tribes in the region and were able to settle on the west bank of the Rhine.

By AD 413 the Burgundiones were recognized by Rome as an allied state, which essentially meant Rome could do nothing about their presence and hoped to make use of their warriors rather than fighting them. The tribe gradually moved westwards and became prominent in the politics of the dying Western Roman Empire. The Burgundian king Gundobad became a general in what passed for a Roman Army towards the end of the fifth century AD, but was defeated by Clovis I of the Franks.

ABOVE: **A late nineteenth-century engraving of Germanic tribesmen and Huns on the march some time in the fourth–sixth century.**

Pushed north – away from the Narbonne region – by the Ostrogoths, the Burgundians retained a kingdom around Lyons and Dijon until AD 534, when they were subjugated by the Franks. After this, Burgundy became a Frankish possession but remained an important player in the politics of Francia long after its people lost their Germanic tribal identity.

The Gepids are grouped by Roman writers among the Gothic tribes and probably shared a common origin. They eventually migrated into Dacia and attempted to settle south of the Danube but were repulsed. The Gepids were subjugated by the Huns but fought against them after the death of Attila to regain their independence. Their kingdom was brought down by an alliance of the Lombards and the Avars, ceasing to exist after AD 567.

The Saxons occupied an area of northern Germania close to the North Sea coast and became notorious in Roman times for piracy and coastal raiding. Their defeat at the hands of the Roman commander Carausius in AD 285–286 triggered a curious incident in which Carausius was accused of profiteering from the campaign. If true, this would hardly be unusual in the Roman world, but Carausius faced execution if found guilty. Instead, he declared himself ruler of an independent province of Britain. Creating a navy out of local tribesmen, Carausius was successful for a few years but was assassinated in AD 293.

Saxon power declined after this, with some tribes migrating into Britain and others retaining their traditional homelands. They were not as greatly affected by the Hunnish invasion as many other tribes, but neither did they exert great influence on the Continent. Those Saxons who migrated to England shaped the history of the era; those who remained in Continental Europe were gradually absorbed by the Franks.

THE ALANS OF THE CAUCASUS ARE ONE OF THE FEW BARBARIAN KINGDOMS OF THE ROMAN ERA TO SURVIVE RIGHT THROUGH THE PERIOD.

The Alemanni, for their part, were a loosely defined group who may or may not have included the Suebi. Roman writings are, as usual, vague and contradictory on the subject. The Alemanni were conquered by the Huns and fought in their armies, and enjoyed only short-lived independence after the death of Attila. In AD 496, the Alemanni were conquered by the Franks under Clovis I. Although their independent history came to an end, their legacy lives on in the French name for Germany.

**THE ALANS**

The Alans, or Alani, are first chronicled in India around 1500 BC, when they called themselves Aryans. This word was descriptive, meaning 'civilized'; it may have been used by various different and possibly unrelated groups. Be that as it may, the ancestors of the Alans migrated eastwards and established a homeland in the Caucasus, where they encountered the people who would become the Bulgars.

The Alans also established populations elsewhere, notably along the Danube. They were known to the Roman Empire as early as the first century BC, although Roman writers are typically unclear on the identity of any particular group. The Alans of the Caucasus were subjugated by the Huns, serving them as allied forces. This took many Alan tribes westwards into

Europe, where their history became intertwined with other tribes in the same geographical area.

Other Alan tribes retreated to remote areas and eventually returned to regain an independent homeland in the Caucasus after the defeat of Attila. Their kingdom endured into the Middle Ages, although at times they were subject peoples of the Khazars. The Alans outlasted their Khazar overlords, whose power was broken by forces from Kiev in AD 965, only to be conquered again by the Mongols. By that time, of course, the 'Dark Ages' were over. Thus, the Alans of the Caucasus are one of the few barbarian kingdoms of the Roman era to survive right through the period. Vestiges of the Alan culture continue to re-assert themselves today.

## THE BULGARS

The Bulgars became known to European historians as a nomadic horse people on the steppes around the Caspian Sea and the River Volga. Their original home may have been somewhere in central Asia. After the defeat of the Huns, the Bulgars settled around the Sea of Azov, from where they raided the Byzantine Empire when they were not employed by it as mercenaries.

LEFT: Marcus Aurelius Mausaeus Valerius Carausius declared himself emperor over the Roman territories of Britannia and northern Gaul. To secure his power he seized the Roman fleet at Boulogne, using it to control the waters around Britain.

ABOVE: John Scylitzes produced a chronicle of the reigns of Byzantine emperors in the ninth to eleventh centuries. It is one of the few surviving primary sources dealing with Byzantium in that period.

The Bulgars came into conflict with the Avars in the second half of the sixth century AD and were greatly diminished but resurged under the leadership of Kubrat to create a short-lived state. After Kubrat's death around AD 642, the Bulgars fragmented into five factions. One of these went west with the Lombards, whereas others joined the Avars and the Khazars. The Volga Bulgars gained control over a region important to trade on the River Volga and survived until conquered by the Mongols in the 1200s.

The modern state of Bulgaria gains its name from the Bulgars who migrated there and created an empire that allied itself with Byzantium. Over time, the Bulgars mingled with the people of the region, who were mostly of Slavic or Thracian descent, and embraced Christianity. The Bulgar state survived until the

# ARYAN

THE TERM 'ARYAN' is quite distinct from 'Arian', which refers to a form of Christian belief. Aryan meant 'civilized' or 'superior' and was used by some peoples in a rather self-congratulatory way to indicate their inherent superiority over those they considered uncivilized barbarians. The term, like many other such words, was hijacked during the twentieth century and it now has unpleasant connotations that are entirely unconnected with its original use.

eleventh century, when it became part of the Byzantine Empire, and reappeared later. Its latest resurgence was at the beginning of the twentieth century, when Bulgaria became independent from the Ottoman Empire.

## FROM TRIBES TO KINGDOMS

By the AD 600s, most of the tribal groups of the late Roman era had fallen by the wayside, but kingdoms had emerged that would become known to modern history. These were no longer barbarian tribes but settled people who built cities and constructed great works of stone. The barbarian origins of these states remained evident in some aspects of their culture, notably energy and ferocity, but this was not a Dark Age of wanton destruction; it was the foundation of a new era.

The barbarian kingdom period saw the beginnings of modern Europe, in which peoples settled where they are found today. Language evolved and became regionalized as each kingdom coalesced, adding words and idioms from Latin to the languages brought by the new arrivals. This accounts for the similarities in many modern languages: Francia, Italy and Iberia were all populated by people who had spoken Latin for many decades when the conquerors arrived. The melding of existing and invader languages began the evolution of modern French, Italian and Spanish.

The Franks ultimately emerged as victors from the turbulence of the Volkswanderung, establishing a powerful state that would dominate the affairs of Europe. Yet this was not without compromises; Francia was subdivided and not always internally peaceful. Other states lost their name and some of their culture but emerged onto the medieval stage under a new identity. There was no medieval kingdom of Ostrogothia or Vandalia, but the influences of these people on the development of medieval Europe was profound nonetheless.

BELOW: **King Charles II of Francia was also king of Italy and held a position we would now refer to as Holy Roman Emperor. 'Roman' in this context meant 'civilized people of Europe' rather than a continuation of the original Roman Empire.**

3

# BRITAIN

The British Isles saw a series of invasions dating all the way back to the retreat of the glaciers at the end of the last Ice Age. Each successive wave of new arrivals brought their culture and language, sometimes displacing previous occupants of a territory. It was not until the Norman Conquest that a unified Britain began to become a possibility.

As the glaciers retreated, hunter-gatherers moved into the British Isles over a land bridge from Europe, which was gradually inundated. A similar bridge may have allowed movement into Ireland until rising sea levels prevented further movement. Once the British Isles were no longer connected to the mainland, local cultures began to diverge from those of Europe. However, this was not a condition of complete isolation.

Crossing the narrow seas to Europe was no small endeavour, but the tribes of the British and European coasts remained in contact with one another. Trade brought more than goods and precious metals; ideas and cultural elements were exchanged

OPPOSITE: A fifteenth-century depiction of the Roman invasion of Britain, showing plate-armoured soldiers armed with medieval weapons. There was no scientific study of the past in that era, and a tendency to assume that things had always been more or less the same.

with every trading expedition, while raids taught the tribes about changes in weaponry and warfare occurring elsewhere.

By the time the Romans first ventured into the British Isles, much of the region was occupied by Celtic tribes who had arrived much earlier and displaced the current occupants. Like the Celts of the continent, the Celtic Britons were loosely organized as tribes and tribal confederations rather than unified states, and were at odds with one another as often as they stood together.

The Roman conquest of Britain was a mix of politics, economics and force – the typical Roman way, in short. Some tribes actively sought to join the empire or saw which way the wind was blowing and became allies rather than be conquered. Others fought or tried to hold the newcomers at arm's length, but in the end what is now England was subjugated and began to become Romanized.

IN SOME CASES, THOSE WHO REBELLED AGAINST THE EMPIRE WERE OFFERED THE CHANCE TO SERVE IN A DISTANT PROVINCE AS AN ALTERNATIVE TO EXECUTION.

It is debatable whether Roman explorers or soldiers ever set foot in Ireland, but they certainly tried to conquer Scotland. This was never more than partially successful; the Roman writer Tacitus wrote admiringly of the Caledonians' courage and ferocity. He compared them to the noble and independent Gauls of the Continent before the Roman Empire subjugated them, and noted that although they could be beaten in battle – repeatedly – they would simply vanish into the countryside and come back later. So long as there were half a dozen Caledonians left to stand together, Tacitus suggested, the Roman Empire would never control their homeland.

This sentiment may have been echoed at the highest levels of government. The first permanent fortifications on the empire's borders were along Gask Ridge in southern Scotland. The more famous walls of Hadrian and Antoninus, built later, were an admission that the empire had reached its maximum extent in the British Isles. The walls alone were not sufficient to keep the Caledonians out of Roman Britain; they were part of a package of measures including the cultivation of good relations with tribes to the north who could act as a buffer zone.

## POST-ROMAN BRITAIN

During the Roman era, the tribes of what would become England became Romanized to varying degrees. This also meant being exposed to a wide range of cultural influences. The Roman Army recruited personnel from all over the known world for its legions and auxiliary regiments. In some cases, those who rebelled against the empire were offered the chance to serve in a distant province as an alternative to execution. This happened to a regiment of Sarmatian cavalry thought by some to be a possible origin of the legend of King Arthur's knights.

Some soldiers and officials stayed after their service was over, marrying into the local population and bringing their children up in a Romano-British style. Other influences were more a matter of habit; the Roman way of doing things was efficient and effective and after the empire collapsed there was no real need to reinvent techniques for constructing buildings or conducting commerce. Thus a Romanesque way of life continued in Britain even after its abandonment by the collapsing empire.

The period after 410, when Emperor Honorius instructed the people of Britain to 'look to their own defence', is a candidate for the title of a Dark Age. Few writings survive, and there was certainly a great deal of turbulence and unrest. Cities declined and there was a move towards building in wood rather than stone, along with re-occupation of traditional Celtic hill forts.

ABOVE: **A wall is only an obstacle if it is defended, but an efficient system of messengers ensured reinforcements could be sent to any threatened section of Hadrian's Wall. Any force that got past would trigger a large-scale response from bases behind the wall.**

# THE LEGEND OF KING ARTHUR

THE LEGEND OF KING Arthur evolved over the centuries. A war leader – not a king – named Arthur is named in early writings as the hero of the Battle of Mount Badon. Later scholarship put forward other candidates for the origins of the legend, including post-Roman cavalry commanders and tribal kings. By the time Geoffrey of Monmouth wrote his *Historia Regum Brittanniae* around 1136, the legend had grown into the beginnings of the 'modern' King Arthur story.

Geoffrey of Monmouth's work was partly based on the *Historia Brittonum*, tracing the lineage of King Arthur and various real figures back to a Trojan/Roman hero named Brutus by way of all manner of imaginary personages. Not surprisingly, Geoffrey of Monmouth's Arthur tale (like later versions) is riddled with anachronisms and concepts borrowed from Welsh mythology.

The legend of King Arthur retains its popularity, but despite periodic attempts to reconstruct the 'real King Arthur story' it remains little more than a fiction spun out of fragmentary historical records, which were themselves of dubious veracity.

ABOVE: It is likely that King Arthur is an entirely mythological construct, inspired by a number of historical figures.

It is known – and hardly surprising – that Roman coins remained in circulation and that little or no new currency was issued. Trade with the Continent seems to have increased in the short term and continued to include a mix of staple goods and luxuries. It may well have seemed in the early fifth century that the empire was going through a rough patch but would be back in force at some point. However, by the end of the century it was clear that the people of Britain were on their own. Many elements of Celtic culture re-emerged from under the Roman veneer. Old tribal divisions and new factions caused the people of Britain to break up into regional polities with their own leaders and conflict was inevitable. In addition to fighting one another, the Britons were under pressure from the north, in the form of Pictish raiders, and from Germanic tribes landing in the southeast and occupying territory there.

OLD TRIBAL DIVISIONS AND NEW FACTIONS CAUSED THE PEOPLE OF BRITAIN TO BREAK UP INTO REGIONAL POLITIES WITH THEIR OWN LEADERS.

## THE ANGLO-SAXON MIGRATION

The arrival of the Anglo-Saxons in Britain has been described as an 'invasion', which is partially true in the sense that they were for the most part unwanted and there was violence. However, the takeover of southeastern Britain took the form more of a migration than a deliberate attack. The new arrivals were Saxons, Angles and Jutes for the most part, migrating across the

BELOW: Despite entreaties from the British people to stay and protect them, the Roman military was withdrawn from Britain by Emperor Honorius.

southern extents of the North Sea from what is now Denmark, northern Germany and the Netherlands. They were familiar with these seas, having sailed them as raiders for many years. Some expeditions were coastal raids against targets that may have been hit repeatedly in the past. However, some groups contained families who claimed land to build settlements or drove away the local inhabitants to take over theirs.

The population of the 'Saxon Shore' grew over time, partly from births and partly from additional families arriving. This caused the newcomers to push inland seeking more territory, increasing tension with the Britons and causing violent clashes from time to time. The Saxons were not the only threat facing the rulers of the Britons, however, so the decision was made to use them rather than fighting with them. Whether this was a Roman idea that had been retained or the rulers of the Britons

BELOW: Hengist and Horsa were the legendary leaders of the Saxon invasion. Horsa was killed in battle in 455, while Hengist became king in what is now Kent.

# VORTIGERN

LITTLE IS KNOWN FOR sure about this period of history. Vortigern is named as Gwrtheyrn in early Welsh writings and features in largely fictional works such as the *Historia Brittonum*, which forms an early part of the legend of King Arthur. Vortigern does appear to have been a historical figure, although the events surrounding his life are heavily distorted by the bias of early chroniclers and the imagination of later ones.

Among the works that do survive are those of Gildas, who was writing in the mid-sixth century. According to Gildas, Vortigern was sufficiently powerful to call himself High King of the Britons. This does not imply a unified people, however; only that Vortigern placed himself above other rulers among the Britons. It is not clear how widely this was recognized.

ABOVE: King Vortigern hoped to use the Saxon invaders against his other enemies, entering into a treaty with Hengist and Horsa in 449.

came up with it themselves is unclear, but either way the deal went badly awry.

Writings from the time are nearly non-existent, and later sources are patchy and probably highly biased, but it seems that a ruler among the Britons – usually named as Vortigern – granted the Saxons land in return for military service. According to the surviving accounts, in 449 Vortigern arranged for the Saxon leaders Hengist and Horsa to assist him against the Picts. They instead betrayed him, critically weakening his realm in the process. Accounts of these times are unreliable to say the least – one has a war leader named Arthur slaying a huge and oddly precise number of Saxons single-handed with the aid of various holy inscriptions on his weaponry. However, it is certain that the

# THE BATTLE OF BADON HILL

TRADITION HOLDS THAT THE Saxons (and, by inference, the Angles, Jutes and their allied contingents) were heavily defeated at the Battle of Badon Hill around 490–500. There is little clear evidence – the location of the battle site is not known and even the identities of the participants are unclear. Later writers state that a war leader named Arthur, with considerable divine assistance, was responsible for crushing the Saxons, but in reality all that can be said for sure is that the Anglo-Saxon expansion was curtailed for a time and that conflict did occur. It is not beyond the bounds of possibility that there was a 'Battle of Badon Hill' somewhere and that the Anglo-Saxons were dealt a heavy blow they would require decades to recover from.

ABOVE: Hill forts were common in Britain before the Roman invasion, and some were reoccupied after 400. There is debate as to whether they were permanently inhabited or intended as places of refuge.

Saxons established themselves in the early 400s and became part of the British political landscape.

According to some sources, the defence of Britain against the Saxons was then led by Ambrosius Aurelianus, who was of Roman descent. Legend has it that the Saxons suffered a major defeat at the Battle of Badon Hill, but the location and date of this conflict remain debatable. Some sort of victory must have occurred, as the Saxon threat was diminished for a time. However, during the sixth century new waves of Saxons began pushing into the kingdoms of Britain.

## NORTHUMBRIA

As the Germanic invaders settled around the southeastern coasts of England and pushed into nearby lands, native kingdoms were emerging elsewhere. The former Roman capital of northern Britain, Eboracum (York), remained the centre of government after the Roman abandonment of the British Isles. The city itself was in decline, with the population following the general trend towards deurbanization.

Along with the move back to the countryside and a general drop in population numbers, there was a distinct reversion to older tribal ways once the Roman veneer was removed. This happened much more quickly in the north, resulting in the emergence of a 'kingdom of northern Britain' with a Celtic flavour. By 470 the kingdom had fragmented, with the ruler of Eboracum holding a position of leader among multiple kings, without formal authority over them.

One of these kingdoms, Berenaccia (or Bernicia), was overrun by the Angles in 547, and in 559 another Anglian kingdom, Deira, came into being. Up until this point the region had been spared the worst of the troubles caused by Germanic newcomers, although some Saxons had been allowed to settle in what is now

BELOW: The city of Eboracum was founded around 71 as a Roman army camp. Later known as Jorvik and York, the city was for a time a capital, and was a primary objective in military campaigns through the centuries.

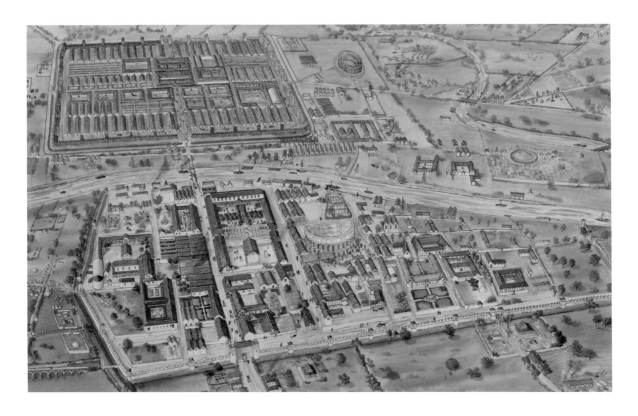

Yorkshire. Eboracum was taken around 580, creating an Anglian kingdom that would eventually become Northumbria.

The name 'Northumbria' comes from 'North of the Humber', the river forming the kingdom's southern frontier. Bernicia (Berenaccia) and Deira were at odds for the first few decades of their existence before being unified by King Aethelfrith of Bernicia in 604. This did not prevent internal divisions from weakening the kingdom at times, which Aethelfrith tried to counter by resettling some of his Deiran subjects in Bernicia. External threats were plentiful, notably the expanding kingdom of Mercia to the south.

Aethelfrith probably died in 616, leaving the way open for the disinherited Prince Edwin to return from exile in East Anglia. Edwin took control of his native Deira and with it the whole semi-unified kingdom. He proved an able leader and further expanded Northumbria, causing grave concern to his neighbours in Mercia and Wessex.

Records are patchy and sources are divided on where some clashes took place, or even if they happened at all. Conflict certainly occurred, however. After trying to have Edwin assassinated, Mercia turned on its former ally of Wessex and inflicted heavy defeats before marching on Northumbria in alliance with Cadwallon ap Cadfan of Wales.

Edwin was killed and Northumbrian power greatly diminished. His successor, Aethelfrith's son Oswald, was unsuccessful in battle but achieved a different form of victory. Edwin was the first Northumbrian king to become a Christian and was revered as a saint for fighting the pagan Mercians and the Welsh. Oswald was likewise

BELOW: After the battle of Chester in 616, King Aethelfrith ordered the monks who had accompanied his enemies to be put to death. This may have been intended to deprive the enemy of divine support.

# RELIGION IN NORTHUMBRIA

NORTHUMBRIA WAS A MAJOR centre of Christianity, although there were tensions between those who practised 'Celtic' Christianity and those who followed orthodox Roman practice. This led to internal conflict and prompted king Oswiu of Northumbria to organize the Synod of Whitby, which took place in 664. As a result, the kingdom came to follow Roman practice. This had great significance for the development of Christianity to this day – some of the major figures of the early Church might have been Celtic Christians were it not for Oswiu.

BELOW: The Synod of Whitby was a pivotal moment for the Church in Britain. Afterward, the Celtic Church declined and Roman Catholicism came to dominate religion in Britain.

considered a martyr to the faith and these new saints became a rallying point for Northumbrian ambition.

Northumbria again fragmented after the death of Oswald, with his brother Oswiu taking the throne of Bernicia and Deira going to Oswine, son of Edwin's cousin. These relatives then made war upon one another for reasons that are not altogether clear. The cause may have been religious differences, but whatever the cause the outcome was clear; Oswiu assassinated Oswine and reunified Northumbria in 654.

Oswiu then attacked Mercia, killing its king Penda in 655. He took the north of the kingdom as his own possession, granting the remainder to Penda's son Peada. Oswiu briefly held all of Mercia after Peada's death but was eventually driven back to the old borders of Northumbria.

The kingdom of Northumbria is sometimes considered to have begun in 654, with reunification under Oswiu, rather than with its first unification earlier in the century. By 660 it was the most powerful of the kingdoms of Britain. However, power did not equate to stability. Infighting among the powerful families of the kingdom saw a succession of kings take the throne for a short time before being done away with by their rivals.

In 829, weakened by internal division, Northumbria became a possession of Egbert, king of Wessex. By this point the kingdom was beset by Norse raids, which intensified into full-scale invasion. In 867 the rival rulers of Bernicia and Deira managed to stop fighting one another long enough to combine forces against a Norse Army but were defeated at York. Northumbria was at times thereafter a Norse kingdom and at times

## THE ANGLO-SAXON CHRONICLE

MUCH OF WHAT WE know about the post-Roman period in the British Isles comes from the *Anglo-Saxon Chronicle*, a work dating from the ninth century. The contents are by no means a complete history of the period, and are clearly biased at times, but with few other manuscripts surviving the work is of great historical importance.

The other great historical work of the period is the *Ecclesiastical History of the English People*, written by the Venerable Bede. This, unsurprisingly, is mainly concerned with religious matters, making the *Anglo-Saxon Chronicle* the only source relating to many non-religious events.

RIGHT: The creation of multiple copies of the *Anglo-Saxon Chronicle* ensured that the document survived into the modern era.

independent as kings were deposed or died. The cycle ended with the incorporation of Northumbria into the realm of Eadred, king of the English.

## MERCIA

The kingdom of Mercia was, for much of the post-Roman era, the most powerful state south of the River Humber. It was founded by a semi-legendary Germanic figure named Icel, possibly as early as 515, although the date of 527 is more commonly used. Icel and his followers arrived in what today are the Midlands by way of East Anglia and retained holdings there for a while. However, in the 580s and 590s, King Creoda ceded these lands to the Germanic tribes living there; they became the basis of the kingdom of East Anglia.

Mercian expansion resulted in conflict with Northumbria. It is possible – although, as usual, sources are unclear - that Mercian forces were involved in the Battle of Chester in 616, in which a Welsh army (with or without Mercian allies) was defeated by the Northumbrians. By 628 Mercia had made large inroads into Wessex and annexed a great deal of territory, before defeating Northumbria and killing its king, Edwin. Mercian territory expanded at the expense of Northumbria and gains were also made in the west.

The situation did not last, however. A resurgent Northumbria, under the command of the Christian King Oswiu, defeated and killed King Penda of Mercia. Penda's son Peada was allowed to keep half the realm and chose to become a Christian. The victory of Christian Northumbrians

BELOW: **King Penda of Mercia secured independence from Northumbria and formed an alliance with Wessex. He later distanced himself from the West Saxons and took advantage of their defeat by Northumbrian forces to extend his own territory.**

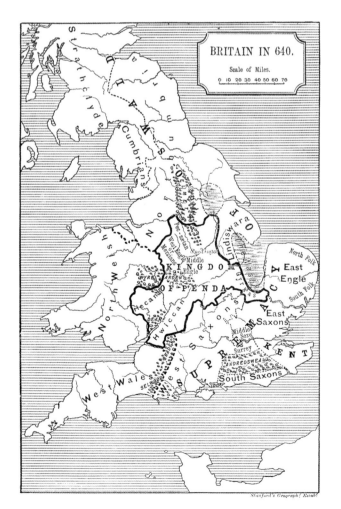

BRITAIN IN 640.

Scale of Miles.

0  10  20  30  40  50  60  70

*Stanford's Geograph! Estab!*

LEFT: **King Offa was recognized as Bretwalda, the high king over all the other rulers of England. His great earthwork (Offa's Dyke) was probably a border marker rather than a fortification.**

over pagan Mercians was taken as a sign that there was strength to be had in the new faith, but Peada did not benefit. He was overthrown by Wulfhere, another son of Penda, who made war upon Wessex.

Wulfhere was defeated at the Battle of Bedwyn in 675, losing territory to Wessex. He died, probably from disease, not long afterward and was succeeded by his brother Aethelred. Aethelred inflicted a significant defeat on the Northumbrians and used this position of strength to negotiate a border agreement. Relations with Northumbria were improved by marriage to Osthryth, daughter of King Oswiu.

Despite plots including the murder of his wife in 697, Aethelred managed to create a period of stability during his reign that outlasted him. Little is known about his successors until Offa took the throne in 757. To do so he overthrew Beornred, apparently without difficulty. Offa took advantage of internal troubles in the kingdom of Kent to launch a successful invasion and conducted highly successful diplomacy.

DESPITE PLOTS INCLUDING THE MURDER OF HIS WIFE IN 697, AETHELRED MANAGED TO CREATE A PERIOD OF STABILITY DURING HIS REIGN THAT OUTLASTED HIM.

Control over Wessex was gained by the marriage of Offa's daughter to King Beorhtric and Mercian ambassadors maintained contact with the powerful Frankish kingdom on the continent. East Anglia was gained without a fight, although there was violence. Depending on the account, Offa may have betrayed King Aethelbert during a royal visit, or may have simply ordered he be slain, after which Mercia controlled East Anglia.

Relations with the Welsh were more troubled. Offa is known to have fought several campaigns against the Welsh, and is best remembered for Offa's Dyke, which is sometimes considered to be a fortification intended to impede Welsh invaders. However, no contemporary record of the dyke's purpose has survived. It may be that it was an extravagant border marker intended to remind potential Welsh invaders they were entering the territory of the most powerful king in Britain.

The reign of Offa was the high point of Mercian fortunes and thereafter it declined. Rebellions, assassinations and external threats diminished Offa's legacy until Mercian power was broken in 825 by an army from Wessex. King Egbert of Wessex took most of Mercia's possessions, leaving only a small remnant that never regained any real significance. Nevertheless, Mercia survived long enough to resist the early Norse invasions of Britain. Further defeat came at the hands of the Great Heathen Army in 874. The Norsemen took part of Mercia and left a puppet king to rule the remainder.

The rise of Alfred the Great as an effective opponent to the Norsemen inspired Mercia to align itself with him. Mercia

## THE BATTLE OF ELLENDUN

THE BATTLE OF ELLENDUN in 825 was a pivotal point in the history of the British Isles, bringing to an end the long rivalry between Mercia and Wessex. Few details of the battle are available and even its location is a matter for conjecture, but it is known that King Egbert of Wessex inflicted a heavy defeat upon Beornwulf of Mercia, gaining territory within Mercia and opening the way to a successful invasion of Sussex, Essex and Kent. East Anglia subsequently broke away from Mercian control as well. Within four years of victory at Ellendun, Egbert was recognized as overlord by the king of Northumbria, making him king of all England.

LEFT: Cerdic, first king of Wessex, is a semi-legendary figure credited with carving out a homeland for his people and establishing the kingdom of the West Saxons. His coronation took place in 532 in Winchester.

suffered greatly from Norse attacks but in doing so contributed to Alfred's victories. The realm gained in strength and resilience after implementing Alfred's defensive strategies, but was eventually annexed by Wessex around 918.

## WESSEX

Wessex was a Saxon kingdom founded in 519 by the chieftain Cerdic, a famous but mysterious figure. Cerdic is mentioned in various histories, often in partial or conflicting accounts. There have been claims that he fought against or even was

TENSIONS WITH NORTHUMBRIA LED TO AN ATTEMPT TO ASSASSINATE KING EDWIN OF NORTHUMBRIA, AFTER WHICH OPEN CONFLICT BROKE OUT.

the legendary King Arthur, but this seems rather unlikely. Very little is known for sure about Cerdic or his life, but the kingdom prospered and grew under its early kings.

Tensions with Northumbria led to an attempt to assassinate King Edwin of Northumbria, after which open conflict broke out. Possibly in alliance with Mercia, forces from Wessex advanced north to meet a Northumbrian army but were soundly defeated. This left Wessex in a weakened state that was exploited by the Mercians, bringing about a period in which Wessex was little more than a collection of small and disorganized realms with little in the way of central authority.

A resurgence began around 674 under a series of kings who reunified Wessex and took back territories lost to Mercia. The last of these was Caedwalla, who treated pagans in his conquered territories harshly and won the favour of the Church. Caedwalla abdicated near the end of his life, choosing to journey to Rome and spend his final days there. Fragmentation followed almost immediately.

Wessex had mixed fortunes until the reign of Beorhtric, who had the support of King Offa of Mercia. Beorhtric took the throne in 786, ruling until 802 when he was poisoned by his wife Eadburh. His realm had benefited from this marriage, bringing close ties to Mercia, and it had enabled Beorhtric to defeat a bid by the dispossessed Egbert to take the throne. With Beorhtric dead, Egbert returned from the court of Charlemagne where he had found refuge. He took the throne with Charlemagne's support and began preparations for war with Mercia.

RIGHT: Caedwalla seized the throne of Wessex in 685, leading a campaign against Sussex, Kent, and – as depicted here – the Isle of Wight. He converted to Christianity and persecuted conquered pagans with zeal.

It was 825 before Egbert was ready, but his preparations had been thorough and he won a series of victories over the Mercians. His territorial gains made Wessex sufficiently powerful that the *Anglo-Saxon Chronicle* names Egbert ruler of Britain. He placed his son Aethelwulf in control of territories won from Mercia after defeating attempts to regain them, while Northumbria recognized Egbert's supremacy without violence.

Egbert died in 839 and was succeeded by Aethelwulf, who was forced to deal with early Norse raids. These intensified over the next decades into full-scale invasion, but initially were small in scope and relatively easy to repel. Aethelwulf was, by all accounts, a wise ruler who understood the value of good advice from trusted people. Some chroniclers consider him too keen to negotiate and compromise, and overly involved in religious matters rather than the affairs of his realm. However, he passed on to his sons a stable and powerful kingdom.

Aethelwulf was succeeded by his son Aethelbald, who died two years after becoming king. The throne passed to his brother Aethelberht, who ruled from 860 to 865 and was, in turn, succeeded by his brother Aethelred. By this time the Norse raids

ABOVE: **King Egbert (left) re-established Wessex as a powerful realm, enabling his son Aethelwulf (or Ethelwolf) (right) to build on his successes. Wessex was thus positioned to become a primary opponent of the Norse invasion of the British Isles.**

ABOVE: The defeat of the Danish leader Guthrum by Alfred the Great curtailed Norse expansion westwards, at least for a time. The measures King Alfred put in place to protect his kingdom arguably prevented England from being completely overrun.

had become an invasion, with large armies on the march. Aethelred achieved some success at times against their incursions but was repeatedly defeated.

## ALFRED THE GREAT

Upon the death of Aethelred in 871, he was succeeded by his brother Alfred. The situation was dire, with most of England under the control of the Norsemen. East Anglia, Mercia and Northumbria had all fallen and Wessex was in severe danger. After fighting a guerrilla campaign for a time, Alfred managed to inflict a severe defeat on the Norsemen at the Battle of Edington in 878. This allowed negotiation of a border agreement, but it is unlikely it would have remained in force if Alfred had not greatly strengthened the defences of his kingdom.

On land, Alfred implemented new rules for military service, enabling him to maintain higher force levels than previously and to get troops to a trouble spot quickly. To impede raids, he created a system of fortified towns called burghs. These would not withstand the assault of a major army but would be an obstacle to a large raiding party. This deprived the Norsemen of easy targets and created fortified bases for Alfred's army to operate from.

The threat of landings on the coast or penetrations inland using rivers was mitigated by a fleet of ships. These were

# ANGLO-SAXON WARRIORS

ANGLO-SAXON WARRIORS fought on foot in a typically Germanic style. A nobleman or king would have a handful of housecarls – professional warriors who would be equipped with the best armour and weapons they could get. The remainder of a force was raised as needed, although individuals might be quite experienced in battle even if they were not warriors by profession.

Spears and axes were the preferred battlefield weapons, along with javelins. A sword or seax – essentially a very large knife – or perhaps a smaller dagger would be carried as a secondary weapon. Most combatants had only a shield for protection, but wealthier men would use mail armour and a helmet if they could afford it.

Tactics were basic, with leaders showing an example and individuals demonstrating their courage by daring feats. An initial exchange of javelins and arrows was followed by a charge by one or both sides, with the issue decided by a violent mêlée. In such circumstances, the casualties among whichever side broke first would be much higher than in an inconclusive skirmish.

BELOW: Anglo-Saxon warriors were, for the most part, simply equipped. The spear remained the primary battlefield weapon.

not intended for long, open-water voyages like those of the Norsemen and could optimize combat capability over seaworthiness. The force proved effective in action, limiting the ability of the Norsemen to raid where they pleased and draw off Alfred's forces. Instead of fruitlessly chasing raiders who were already on the way back to their ships, Alfred could concentrate on dealing with major threats.

Alfred the Great was seen as a defender not only of the English people but of the Christian faith from the pagan Norsemen. This was a rallying point for those who might have political differences with the English king, and with a common enemy came the beginnings of national unity. Alfred was also a lawgiver who understood the need for knowledge and study among those who would rule effectively. His legend was no doubt inflated by his chroniclers, but his example of piety, wisdom and organizational ability was emulated by many who came after.

ALFRED THE GREAT WAS SEEN AS A DEFENDER NOT ONLY OF THE ENGLISH PEOPLE BUT OF THE CHRISTIAN FAITH FROM THE PAGAN NORSEMEN.

## EAST ANGLIA

The kingdom of East Anglia came into being in around 571. The Angles had gradually gained control of the region over the previous century, along with a large number of Saxons who had settled there in late Roman times. The union of the North and South Folk created a powerful kingdom whose fortunes waxed and waned over the years. The Angles were prosperous and could afford to bury rich grave goods with their kings and nobles. Burial mounds such as that found at Sutton Hoo in Suffolk have given modern scientists an insight into the way of life and intricate metalworking skills of the Angles and their Germanic kin.

The interplay between 'native' kingdoms and the new arrivals from the continent was far more complex than a simple 'native British versus Anglo-Saxons' split. East Anglia was a player in the political game of the era and its alliances transcended a simplistic

OPPOSITE: This helmet formed part of a treasure buried in the seventh century with a notable individual, probably a king, at Sutton Hoo in East Anglia. The wealth of the burial site suggests a powerful and prosperous kingdom.

cultural divide. Edwin, future king of Northumbria, was given
refuge in East Anglia. His enemy, Aethelfrith of Northumbria,
tried to bribe and coerce the Anglians into killing Edwin, but
ultimately they chose instead to assist him in defeating Aethelfrith
and taking the Northumbrian crown.

East Anglia benefited from the gratitude of Edwin, but this
brought new problems. Eorpwald, king of the East Angles,
was persuaded to convert to Christianity, which did not please

RIGHT: Edwin of
Northumbria married
Aethelburgh, a princess
from Kent who was a
Christian. Through her
influence, Edwin was
converted; his baptism
by the missionary
Paulinus made
Northumbria officially
a Christian kingdom.

all of his subjects. He was killed by his brother Richtbert, who returned the realm to paganism until Sigeberht, another brother of Eorpwald, took the throne and returned the East Angles to Christianity – officially, at least. Changes in religious practice at the local level took place far more slowly than the baptism of a king.

In 645, another dispossessed king found refuge in East Anglia. This was Cenwalh of Wessex, driven from his throne by King Penda of Mercia. Religious sources of the period make much of the fact that Cenwalh was baptized while in East Anglia and it may be that the Anglians were keen to assist a fellow Christian against the pagan Mercians. However, there was undoubtedly a great deal of self-interest about this arrangement – an expanded Mercia was an increased threat to its neighbours.

By 654, East Anglia had suffered repeated defeats at the hands of King Penda of Mercia, and – no doubt reluctantly – became an ally in Penda's wars against Northumbria. East Anglian and Mercian forces were defeated by King Oswiu of Northumbria in 654 or 655, resulting in a further decline of Anglian power. By the end of the century, East Anglia was a governed territory of Mercia, a situation that continued until the 820s.

Under King Aethestan, East Anglia began making attempts to free itself from Mercian governance in 821, but it was not until 825 – when Mercia was heavily defeated by Wessex – that success was achieved. By 827, East Anglia was once again an independent state, though closely aligned with and subordinate to Wessex. By this time, raids by the Norsemen were becoming an increasing problem. The situation changed radically

ABOVE: Coins issued in the reign of King Aethelstan proclaimed him king of all England. Strict laws and close control of the mints were intended to strengthen the economy.

THE SITUATION CHANGED IN 865 WHEN AN ARMY OF NORSEMEN ARRIVED AS CONQUERORS RATHER THAN RAIDERS, AND EAST ANGLIA WAS THE FIRST TO FALL.

# THE MIDDLE ANGLES

LARGE NUMBERS OF SETTLERS, many of them Angles, moved into the region between the Thames and the Trent, becoming known as the Middil Engli, or Middle Angles.

The region formed part of the kingdom of Mercia, but the Middle Angles maintained a cultural identity of their own. They were therefore one of several groups that played a significant part in the wars and events of the Dark Ages without being mentioned as a kingdom or state.

in 865 when an army of Norsemen arrived as conquerors rather than raiders. East Anglia was the first to fall, after which the army turned north into Northumbria. Thereafter, East Anglia was a Danish kingdom.

### KENT, ESSEX AND SUSSEX

Kent, or Cantware, was taken over by Germanic tribes, notably Jutes, in the mid-450s. Although some settlers were already in place, the Germanic takeover of Kent began with Hengist and Horsa, leaders of the Angles, who were invited to fight for King Vortigern against his Pictish enemies. Hengist and Horsa seem to have initially done so, but then come to the conclusion that the Britons made better victims than paymasters.

Although Horsa was killed, Hengist drove the Britons out of Kent by 457 and was joined by a wave of Jutes seeking a new home. Some Saxons and other Germanic people also settled in Kent, which became the earliest of the Anglo-Saxon kingdoms. Their expansion was resisted by forces under Ambrosius Aurelianus, limiting the territory they could claim.

The traditional date for the founding of the kingdom of Kent is 488. It appears that, after a widespread campaign of plunder, there was a period of consolidation and population growth, during which little is recorded about the people of Kent. However, it is likely that they were involved in the affairs of neighbouring kingdoms, notably Essex. Like East Anglia, the area that became the kingdom of Essex had been settled by

LEFT: The sight of Norse longships inspired dread around the coasts of England. One or two ships might be a trading expedition, but a fleet meant that a raid or even an invasion was in progress.

Saxons since Roman times. Some had come as foederati; others migrated from the continent and joined the existing communities or claimed new areas. The exact founding date of the kingdom is open to some debate, although the figure of 527 is often quoted. It is possible that the region was a more or less unified state before this, under the auspices of Kent.

The kingdom of the East Seaxe (Essex) reached natural frontiers to the north and controlled the region of the Midil Seaxe, possibly through local sub-rulers. Essex and Kent remained closely related; indeed, were it not for the barrier of the Thames between them, they might have been a single kingdom.

Essex became a Mercian possession in the early 800s and, after the eclipse of Mercia in 825, Essex became subordinate to King Egbert of Wessex. Kent met a similar fate, initially at the hands of Offa of Mercia. The region rebelled against Mercian rule in the 770s and may have achieved brief independence but was reconquered in 785. After 825 Kent, like Essex, was dominated by Wessex.

The east of England was increasingly beset by Norse raids, which intensified into invasion. Despite resistance from the local population and the Wessex-led kingdom of England, it proved impossible to dislodge the invaders. Norse settlers were granted land in East Anglia in a peace deal that might have lasted but for the arrival of another Norse Army. Essex became part of the Norse-controlled region known as the Danelaw, while Kent became part of the kingdom of England.

The kingdom of the South Seaxe (Sussex) followed a similar pattern. According to the *Anglo-Saxon Chronicle*, the kingdom was founded in 477 by Germanic invaders who drove out or conquered the local population. Successive waves of migration increased the Saxon population of the kingdom, but little is recorded about its history. This might be taken as evidence that the semi-legendary Battle of Badon Hill, or some analogue to it, did occur. Saxon expansion was more or less halted around 500. A major defeat might account for this sudden reversal of fortunes.

> NORSE SETTLERS WERE GRANTED LAND IN EAST ANGLIA IN A PEACE DEAL THAT MIGHT HAVE LASTED BUT FOR THE ARRIVAL OF ANOTHER NORSE ARMY.

In 607, Wessex began making war on Sussex, forcing the South Seaxe into an alliance with Mercia. This allowed the kingdom to survive and, as the power of Wessex waned, Sussex enjoyed a revival of its fortunes. It was not to last; as Wessex in turn resurged, Sussex was subjugated. Independence was regained in the early 700s, but the kingdom again fell – this time to Offa of Mercia in 772. The final period of South Saxon independence began around 796 after the death of Offa, but

## THE HEPTARCHY

THE SEVEN KINGDOMS OF **Anglo-Saxon Britain (East Anglia, Essex, Kent, Mercia, Northumbria, Sussex and Wessex) are commonly referred to as the Heptarchy.**

**Their relative power changed over the years, with some at times subjugated by others. All were eventually absorbed into the emerging kingdom of England.**

LEFT: The kingdoms of England and Wales during the ninth century. Despite claims of high kingship over all England, the realms remained largely independent unless subjugated and directly ruled.

after the events of 825 Sussex once more became a possession of Wessex. Thereafter, it was part of the Wessex-dominated kingdom of England.

## THE CELTIC KINGDOMS OF MAINLAND BRITAIN
Relatively little – even compared to the sketchy data available on the main English kingdoms – is known about the Celtic kingdoms of the British Isles. Much of what is recorded comes from religious figures visiting Ireland, Scotland and the west of mainland Britain, often writing with a heavy bias about matters they did not truly understand.

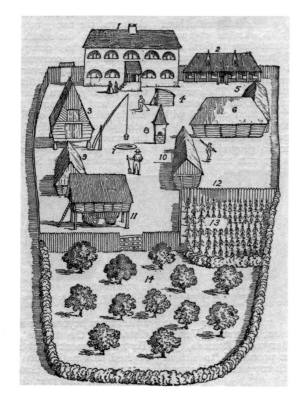

ABOVE: Most of the Celtic peoples of the British Isles used a communal homestead constructed along these lines: 1) common dwelling house; 2) summer dwelling house; 3) granary; 4) common goose-house; 5) cows' and goats' house; 6) shed for making plum brandy; 7) well; 8) common oven; 9) stables; 10) swine stall; 11) loft for maize; 12) paling; 13) maize; 14) orchard.

The Celtic people of mainland Britain were driven westwards by the Anglo-Saxons into Wales, Devon and Cornwall. There, they mingled with other Celts already resident. The people of Devon and Cornwall, largely descended from the Dumnonii tribe, had not vigorously resisted the Roman invasion and were absorbed into the empire quite peaceably. This meant that they were governed lightly and lost less of their Celtic character than those tribes that were heavily subjugated.

Therefore, the people of Devon and Cornwall were affected less by the Roman arrival and departure than others in England, and emerged from the Roman era as the kingdom of Dumnonia. Controlling Devon, Cornwall and part of Somerset, the kingdom played a relatively small part in the affairs of the rest of England, but did come into conflict with Wessex on several occasions. This eventually led to the conquest of most of the kingdom by Egbert of Wessex in 814, although Dumnonia attempted to regain its independence in 825 and again in 838. Final defeat came at the Battle of Hingston Down in 838, despite an alliance with Norsemen based in Ireland.

The Brythonic people of Wales, on the other hand, remained independent of England until long after the Norman invasion. In the years following the Roman abandonment of Britain, the people of Wales reverted to a more tribal way of life, much as in other areas. Initially, territories were small and conflict was common, with the victors enlarging their holdings over time.

By the early 600s, the small territories of northern Wales had coalesced into the kingdom of Gwynedd. Its king from 625 was Cadwallon ap Cadfan, who successfully halted the expansion of Northumbria. Up to that point the Northumbrians had been advancing west, driving the Celtic inhabitants from northern mainland England.

In alliance with the neighbouring Welsh kingdom of Powys, Gwynedd's forces had been defeated at Chester in 613 and initially Cadwallon was little more successful. Indeed, he was driven to Anglesey and ultimately across the Irish Sea but, according to some sources at least, managed to raise a new army and returned to the British mainland by way of Dumnonia, where he helped defeat Penda of Mercia.

Now in alliance with the Mercians, in 633 Cadwallon invaded Northumbria. This brought about the Battle of Hatfield Chase, where King Edwin of Northumbria, was killed and the subsequent fragmentation of Northumbria into Deira and Bernicia. Cadwallon was defeated and killed at the Battle of Heavenfield by Northumbrian (mainly Deiran) forces.

With the Northumbrian threat to Wales curtailed, at least for the time being, the Brythonic people looked mainly to their own affairs. Conflict with Mercia was common, as were internal clashes. Wales was never united, although some rulers came close. Rhodri the Great, king of Gwynedd, succeeded in gaining control over Powys and Seisyllwg by 871. Although referred to as 'king of the Britons' and indeed 'king of Wales', he did not rule the whole of Wales nor all of its people.

By the 900s, Norse raids were becoming increasingly common, largely due to the establishment of bases in Ireland and the Isle of Man. Despite these troubles, Gruffydd ap Llywelyn finally managed to create a unified kingdom around 1057. His reign over it was short, however; he was defeated in 1063 by an English Army under Harold Godwinson and killed soon afterward.

## THE PICTS

The Picts of Scotland remain a mysterious people. Roman writers knew very little about

BELOW: The battle of Heavenfield, in 633 or 634, is believed to have taken place just north of Hexham, close to Hadrian's Wall. Today a marker stands on the presumed site where Oswald defeated the joint Welsh-Mercian army.

them and what they did know was coloured by assumptions that may not have been valid. It is highly likely that the Picts were the descendants of the original inhabitants of what is now Scotland, intermixed with Celtic people who arrived later. Their society seems to have been similar to that of the British tribes at the time of the Roman invasion and was changed less by the Roman occupation as a result of successful resistance to encroachment and conquest.

The kingdom of Northumbria was more successful than the Roman Empire against the Picts, although by the 600s the Pictish people had been converted to Christianity and their culture had begun to change more than it ever had in Roman times. Under pressure from the Scots, who had come from Ireland to occupy the west coast, the Picts also found themselves in conflict with Northumbria.

In 670 the Picts suffered a defeat at the Battle of Two Rivers, after which Brude Mac Bile came to power. He was a cousin of the king of Northumbria, who may or may not have assisted his rise to power on condition of receiving tribute. Whether or not that was the case, Brude Mac Bile chose instead to raid Northumbria while increasing his power by subjugating Pictish lands as far afield as the Orkney Isles.

Northumbria responded with what appears to have been an over-confident campaign against the Picts, who inflicted a major defeat at Dun Nechtain in 685. According to the Venerable Bede, the Picts retreated in the face of Northumbrian attacks, drawing their force into difficult terrain before counterattacking. This victory ended the Northumbrian threat to the Pictish kingdom until the end of the century.

BELOW: A Pictish slab dating from the eighth century found at Aberlemno, in Angus. Little is known about the Picts as they left no written records – only tantalizing carvings like this one, hinting at battles and other great events.

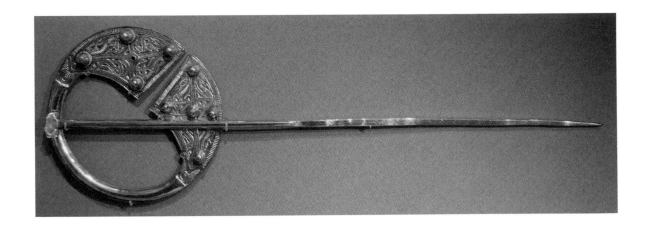

In 698 another Northumbrian invasion was repulsed, ushering in two decades of peace that was shattered by internal conflict over whether to follow Celtic Christian or Roman Catholic religious practices. A decade of infighting was finally brought to a close by finding someone else to fight. The Picts invaded the Scottish kingdom of Dalriada and took their capital, Dunadd, in 736. Little was written about the Pictish kingdom for the next few decades until the 780s, when the Picts and Scots were first united under a single crown.

By the 800s, the people of what would become Scotland were fending off increasingly intense Norse raids and encroachments from England. This pressure caused the Pictish and Scottish people to become increasingly a single culture. There are no mentions of Picts in the chronicles after 900. By this time the banner of Scotland, the Saltire, was in use and the joint realm was known as Alba. This identity was short-lived; by 1094 King Duncan II would be referred to as king of Scotland.

ABOVE: The Celtic people were noted for their intricate functional and decorative metalwork. This ring brooch dates from eight-century Ireland.

BY THE 800S, THE PEOPLE OF WHAT WOULD BECOME SCOTLAND WERE FENDING OFF INCREASINGLY INTENSE NORSE RAIDS AND ENCROACHMENTS FROM ENGLAND.

## IRELAND AND THE SCOTS

The early inhabitants of Ireland were joined by waves of new arrivals, mostly of Celtic origin, who created a society along tribal lines. Minor kings ruled small areas, owing loose allegiance to a higher tier of overlords, and finally to the kings of the major

ABOVE: **Fergus Mór mac Eirk is a legendary figure, with few reliable sources referring to him. Certainly Irish people migrated into western Scotland, but whether Fergus led them is questionable.**

regions. Conflict was common and the fortunes of the major provinces rose and fell. One of the five great provinces of Ireland, Meath, lay more or less in the centre and was the seat of the High King who – in theory at least – ruled over all other kings in Ireland.

Munster, in the southwest, was formed from three smaller kingdoms. To its east lay the largest of the provinces, Leinster, and to the north, Connaught. The northeast of Ireland was the province of Ulster, which maintained links with what would become Scotland by way of a short sea crossing. Ireland in general and Leinster in particular – for obvious geographical reasons – was involved in the affairs of the Celtic people of the British mainland, sometimes warring with the Welsh kingdoms and often giving refuge to Welsh leaders forced to flee by their enemies.

According to tradition, this was the reason for the establishment of Irish kingdoms in what would become Scotland. Fergus Mór mac Eirk of the Dál Riata tribe of northeastern Ireland led his followers across the narrow sea to Scotland and set up a kingdom known as Dál Riata (or Dalriada) there. However, there is little archaeological evidence to support this. It does seem that Irish Gaels crossed into Scotland as well as northern England and Wales, and that some settled in or mingled with the local population over a long period. This resulted in a culture with a different regional flavour to the Pictish society elsewhere.

These Irish migrants were known as Scoti (or Scotti), although the term originally applied to all Gaelic people rather than those residing on the British mainland. Their kingdom of Rheged, in northwestern England and southern Scotland, was overrun by Northumbria by 730, whereas Dalriada endured into the ninth

# THE MATTER OF SCOTLAND

SCOTLAND, LIKE ENGLAND AND FRANCE, has a body of classic literature chronicling its ancient past and the lineage of its legendary kings into recorded times. Known as 'the matter of Scotland', this body of work weaves a wondrous but rather unlikely tale.

According to this version of events, Scota was the daughter of an Egyptian pharaoh who married a man from Babylon named Fénius Farsaid. Their son founded the Gaelic race and created its language. Other versions of the tale have the couple leaving Egypt for Spain where their son Mil was born. He led his followers into Ireland, overthrowing the magical Tuatha Dé Danann.

Eventually, the people of Ireland began to name themselves after Scota, as did their kin who moved to what would become Scotland. Thus the Scots can claim their birthright all the way back to the pharaohs of ancient Egypt. Marvellous as it may be, this tale is no more likely to be true than the founding of Britain by the Trojan/Roman Brutus or the legendary Trojan origins of certain Germanic tribes.

century, eventually becoming part of the kingdom of Alba and finally the nation of Scotland.

## ENGLAND AFTER ALFRED

The kingdoms of England followed the practice of electing a king from among suitable candidates rather than following the laws of primogeniture coming into use on the Continent. Therefore, after the death of Aethelred, his brother Alfred was elected king rather than appointing a regent to rule on behalf of Aethelred's young sons.

This was greatly beneficial to the kingdom. Not only did Alfred succeed in driving back the Norsemen, he also fostered learning and training for governmental officials, implemented a body of law and began the creation of an official history of the kingdom. This would become the *Anglo-Saxon Chronicle*. Alfred's wisdom in ensuring there were several copies distributed at

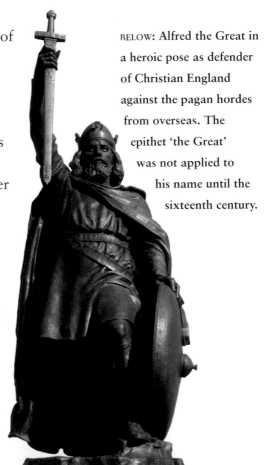

BELOW: Alfred the Great in a heroic pose as defender of Christian England against the pagan hordes from overseas. The epithet 'the Great' was not applied to his name until the sixteenth century.

ABOVE: **Edward the Elder was rightfully elected as Alfred's successor, but faced a military challenge from Aethelwald. His wise policy of consolidation cemented his successes and increased the resilience of his realm.**

centres of learning permitted the *Chronicle* to survive to the present day.

Alfred, who was not known as 'the Great' in his own lifetime, died in 899. He was succeeded by his son, Edward the Elder, though not without dispute. Aethelwald, son of Alfred's predecessor Aethelred, had been passed over for the throne already and now felt that he should become king. There was nothing illegal about Edward's election as king; he had been elected by the Witan, an assembly of the most powerful nobles. This did not stop Aethelwald from seeking assistance in gaining the throne by force.

In 905 Aethelwald, supported by a Norse Army from Northumbria, invaded Edward's kingdom and inflicted a defeat in which Aethelwald was killed. This opened the way for a negotiated peace, but conflict was renewed soon afterward. Edward followed a policy of consolidating his victories, fortifying towns in the manner Alfred the Great had pioneered, and gradually expanded his realm at the expense of the Norse kingdoms. In 920 he received the submission of the northern British kings.

Edward the Elder was succeeded in 924 by his son Aelfweard, whose older brother, Aethelstan, was to be made ruler of Mercia. The use of sub-kings to administer territories within a large kingdom was a tradition dating back hundreds of years, but it may be that Aethelstan did not wish to be subordinate.

Aelfweard was killed just two weeks after his father's death and, although it is not clear if Aethelstan was involved, it does seem likely. Aethelstan then became king of all England.

Aethelstan did away with another of his brothers, Edwin, who was cast adrift in a boat with no food or water. Having thus secured his throne against likely claimants (Aethelstan was convinced Edwin was plotting against him, but this remains debatable), he attempted to make peace with the Norsemen. This resulted in the marriage of his sister Edith to Sithric, the Norse king, at York.

The death of Sithric gave Aethelstan a pretext to annex Northumbria and he further extended his territories in Cornwall with a campaign of conquest. In 937, Aethelstan faced an invasion comprising both Norsemen and Scots. The decisive clash came at the Battle of Brunanburh in 937. Details are few, but

BELOW: The location of the Battle of Brunanburh is open to much debate, as is whether or not the Anglo-Saxons used a force of cavalry. What is clear is that the battle marked a pivotal moment in English history, after which a unified realm began to emerge.

the *Anglo-Saxon Chronicle* states that five kings and seven earls were slain in the fighting. This victory made Aethelstan's position unassailable and marks the point where his realm changed from being a collection of territories to being a single kingdom.

Aethelstan made good marriages for his sisters, securing alliances with the Holy Roman Emperor, the king of France and other notables of the period. By the time of his death in 940, Aethelstan had placed the Anglo-Saxon kingdom of England firmly on the political map of Europe. He was well regarded in his time and afterwards as a just king who did much to support the poor as well as promoting stability within the realm.

Aethelstan was succeeded by his brother Edmund, who entered into an agreement with the Norse ruler of York, Olaf Guthfrithson, that upon the death of either of them the whole country would be ruled by the other. Olaf's death in 944 expanded Edmund's realm into Northumbria and soon afterward he campaigned against Olaf's former allies in Strathclyde.

# DYNASTIC MURDER

MANY HISTORICAL FIGURES HAVE been vilified for doing away with potential rivals, but this was an essential part of statecraft in the era. A disenchanted or dispossessed noble might rouse rebellion and one might be raised in support of someone who had no wish to challenge for the throne. The assassination or execution of rivals or those who stood in the way of ambition was, quite simply, normal behaviour for the ambitious prince of the early medieval period.

Likewise, assassinating an unfriendly ruler to create a political or military advantage was a valid and accepted stratagem. Indeed, an assassination might forestall or at least limit a destructive war or an internal power struggle, which would be to the benefit of those who otherwise might have suffered. Modern sensibilities might be offended by a ruler who cold-bloodedly murdered his way to the throne, but it could be argued that a ruler without the stomach for state-sanctioned murder was unfit for the task. In any case, those who were unwilling to take such actions were likely to be victims of those who were. Eliminating the opposition by any means necessary was at times nothing more or less than a survival measure.

LEFT: **King Edmund survived the many dangers of his position – war and the possibility of assassination, among others – only to be stabbed to death in an easily avoidable incident of his own making.**

Edmund was also active in the politics of the Continent, assisting Louis IV in taking the French throne, but he came to an untimely end in a drunken brawl with a man named Liofa whom Edmund had outlawed some years earlier. Enraged at seeing Liofa at the festival of St Augustine, Edmund attacked him and was stabbed to death.

These incidents encapsulate the character of monarchy in the tenth century. Edmund, sometimes known as 'the magnificent', greatly expanded his power, put down rebellions and had a hand in dictating the fate of other realms, yet was not above assaulting a man at a feast when his temper got the better of him.

AETHELSTAN WAS WELL REGARDED IN HIS TIME AND AFTERWARDS AS A JUST KING WHO DID MUCH TO SUPPORT THE POOR AS WELL AS PROMOTING STABILITY.

The Anglo-Saxon kingdom of England was well established by the time of Edmund's death in 946. The chief threat at this time was the growing power of the Norse kingdoms. The complex politics of the time put Eric Bloodaxe, a Norse prince, on the throne of Northumbria. Ousted, he later returned to rule again until dislodged a second time. He was finally killed in an ambush that may have been orchestrated by Edred, successor to Edmund as king of England.

By 978, when King Aethelred 'the Unready' took the throne of England, the Norse kingdoms were engaged in further conquests. Aethelred's nickname has little to do with lack of preparedness; it is a corruption of the Anglo-Saxon word for 'ill-advised'. Be that as it may, England was unable to resist the attacks of the Norsemen, and Aethelred began to pay Danegeld – essentially a protection racket on an international scale – to spare his realm from ravage or conquest.

In 1013 Aethelred was overthrown by King Sweyn Forkbeard of Denmark, who ruled England for two years until his death. At this point, Aethelred managed to regain his throne. He died in 1016 and was briefly succeeded by his son Edmund Ironside, at least according to some nobles of the kingdom. A larger proportion supported Cnut (or Canute), son of Sweyn Forkbeard, leading to what might be considered an invasion, a civil war or a monarch putting down a rebellion, depending upon perspective. Edmund Ironside achieved some success in battle but was ultimately defeated by Cnut. The subsequent peace agreement gave Edmund the kingdom of Wessex, but upon his death soon afterward Cnut became undisputed king of England.

ABOVE: **King Cnut's courtiers were prone to flatter him more than he thought appropriate, so Cnut demonstrated that the seas obeyed God, not men, and that his own power was trivial before the Almighty.**

OPPOSITE: **Aethelred the Unready, depicted in a manuscript dating from around 1220. Aethelred's policy of paying Danegeld has been criticized, but the alternative for his people was far worse.**

Cnut is widely portrayed as a fool who thought he could order the tide not to come in, but in fact the incident was quite different to that of the popular story. Cnut chose to demonstrate that he understood how little the power of mortal kings meant beside the majesty of God by ordering the tide to stay out. It did not, of course, and thus Cnut demonstrated his powerlessness before God. What was supposed to be a demonstration of humility before the Almighty passed into folk legend as the act of an egotistical buffoon. Cnut's reign saw the Norse threat to England greatly reduced, partly due to his

RIGHT: Edward the Confessor's sons, if he had had any, would have been among the primary candidates for the throne of England. However, succession was by election rather than automatic succession of the eldest child, so a dispute over the English throne might still have occurred.

EDWARDVS REX. ANGLIÆ

power and partly because he controlled many of those who might otherwise have invaded or raided. However, since he was also king of Denmark after 1018, Cnut's realm was entangled in the complex affairs of Scandinavia. Upon his death in 1035, the throne was intended to pass to his son Harthacnut. However, it was taken by Harthacnut's brother Harald Harefoot, who was initially installed as regent while Harthacnut was campaigning in Denmark. This appears to have caused some bad blood; after Harald's death, Harthacnut had his body disinterred and thrown into a bog.

Harthacnut ascended to the English throne in 1040, but died two years later, at which point the vagaries of dynastic marriages returned the House of Wessex to the throne. Emma of Normandy, wife of the deceased Aethelred the Unready, had married Cnut while he was king of England. This placed her sons Alfred and Edward in line to succeed Cnut. Alfred was taken prisoner and blinded during a visit to England in 1037, dying from his injuries, but Edward survived.

In 1040, Edward was summoned to the court of Harthacnut and, upon his death in 1042, succeeded him to the throne of England. He became known as 'the Confessor' due to his great piety, which may have been taken too far. Although married, he produced no children, leading to some sources stating he had taken a vow of celibacy. Edward came into conflict with his father-in-law, Earl Godwin of Wessex, who initially rose in rebellion but chose to accept exile when it became clear he could not garner enough support to defeat Edward. Such was the power of Earl Godwin that, a year later, in 1052, he arrived back in England at the head of an army and forced the king to accept his return.

Earl Godwin had two sons, Harold and Tostig. When Edward the Confessor died in 1066 leaving a disputed succession, both put themselves forward as candidates for the throne. Harold Godwinson, Earl of Wessex, was selected, but this was disputed by his brother Tostig, who was at the time Earl of Northumbria. However, there was a third candidate – Duke William of Normandy – who was also willing to back up his claim with force. His victory at Hastings in 1066 would usher in a new era of English history.

BELOW: The Battle of Hastings in 1066 brought an end to Anglo-Saxon England, and also to the so-called 'Viking Era'. This was the last occasion upon which the British Isles were successfully invaded.

# 4

# THE CHURCH

Despite attempts at suppression, the Christian Church became
the state religion of the Roman Empire, establishing its position
as the primary faith in Europe. As the early growth and spread
of Christianity was driven by zealous individuals rather than
a coherent programme of expansion, it was inevitable that
differences would emerge in practices and even core beliefs.
Much of the history of the Church has been driven by attempts
to resolve these differences.

THE ROMAN Empire understood the importance
of religion as a tool of statecraft, although some
emperors failed to grasp the implications of certain
actions. By the time of Jesus, Rome had learned that
interfering with the religion of a conquered people, especially
Jews, was liable to trigger a revolt. Harsh taxation and general
oppression could be borne by the Jewish people – not without
resistance, but with dissent falling short of large-scale rebellion.

Even the Roman practice of appointing the high priest – giving

OPPOSITE: **A medieval
depiction of the First
Jewish–Roman War,
or Great Revolt, of AD
66–73. The Jewish leader
and historian Josephus
is being brought before
Roman general (and future
emperor) Vespasian.**

the post to a sympathizer rather than a holy man selected by his own people – was not quite enough to trigger rebellion, but when Emperor Caligula insisted that a statue of himself be placed in every place of worship, the Jewish people rose up in what would become known as the Great Revolt. Caligula was, by his own announcement, a god and placing idols of foreign gods in the holiest of places was simply too much for Jews to accept.

The Great Revolt began in AD 66, with Roman forces initially suffering heavy losses. By AD 70 it had been largely put down, but the ferocity of the Jewish rebels ensured the incident would be well remembered even by its victors. It was clearly undesirable to have a religion spreading within the empire that could serve as a rallying point for further rebellions. An outsider religion was also a challenge to the established Roman faith.

Christians were persecuted within the Roman Empire, although intermittently for the most part. At times it was possible for Christians to hold public office; at others, the conversion of a relative could mean dismissal or even execution for a government figure. Major persecutions took place after the Great Fire of Rome in AD 64 and under Emperor Decius from 250 to 261. The last large-scale persecution was on the orders of Emperor Diocletian in 303. His successor, Constantine, implemented a policy of freedom of religion in the empire.

## THE FIRST COUNCIL OF NICAEA

Given the early history of the Christian religion, it was inevitable that there would be significant differences among

BELOW: Emperor Caligula, depicted here seated between statues of Castor and Pollux, declared himself a god and demanded worship. Some of his subject people could stomach this, but the Jews could not.

# THE CONVERSION OF CONSTANTINE

CONSTANTINE THE GREAT CAME to power during the Tetrarchy, a period when the Roman Empire was ruled by four emperors, each with control over a region. Proclaimed emperor by his army, he faced opposition from Maxentius, who had declared himself emperor in Rome. The night before their decisive clash at the Milvian Bridge over the River Tiber, Constantine dreamed that victory would be his if he followed Christian ways.

Constantine was indeed successful, and became ruler of a temporarily reunified Roman Empire. He moved his capital to the Eastern Roman Empire and implemented a policy of tolerance that eventually permitted Christianity to become the official religion of the empire. His reign saw a resurgence of Roman power and victories over a number of barbarian peoples, which may have assisted in persuading Romans to accept the new state religion.

ABOVE: Constantine the Great at the Milvian Bridge in 312. Like many others, he valued religion for the assistance it could give him in earthly endeavours.

Christian groups. By the time of the Council of Nicaea, held in 325, a formal system of bishops presiding over local religious matters was in place but there was no overall agreement on the practices of the Church. The First Council of Nicaea was called by Emperor Constantine to resolve these differences and to create a unified set of practices throughout the whole of Christendom.

Among the most serious matters facing the Church was the Arian Controversy. A theologian named Arius contended that, contrary to the conventional belief that the Holy Trinity of God the Father, the Son and the Holy Spirit were one being, God

ABOVE: Emperor Constantine convened the Council of Nicaea in the hope of creating a unified body of practice within the Christian Church. Although not entirely successful, the council did agree practices that are still followed today.

alone had existed in the beginning and had called his son into being. This meant that Jesus was not the same as (or an aspect of) God but a separate being of a lower order. The implications of this concept were highly complex and the ideas behind Arianism were unacceptable to conventional Trinitarians.

The Council of Nicaea did not resolve the Arian Controversy as such but it established the Nicene Creed, which followed Trinitarianism. This became the standard for the official Church, with the followers of Arius seen as heretics. Arius and his supporters were exiled but Arianism continued to be practised in many areas. Later councils attempted to resolve the matter with no greater success.

The Arian Controversy came to affect the politics of the emerging states of Europe. Groups that were converted to Christianity may not have been aware at the time that this would involve them in a new set of complications. Those that embraced Nicene Trinitarianism found the Eastern Roman Empire, and later the Byzantine Empire, better disposed to them than those who were converted to Arianism. This, in turn, influenced the support received from the emperor, who at times pressurized kingdoms not to assist fellow Arians against Nicaeans.

## CHRISTIANITY IN POST-IMPERIAL ROME

Nicaean Christianity was declared the official religion of the Roman Empire by Emperor Theodosius in AD 380, by which time the Western Empire was in deep decline. There was no central religious authority at first, although the emperor might consider himself the head of the Church. Several cities were at the time major centres of Christianity, and each might have considered itself the foremost. Jerusalem had a claim as the place where it all started and Rome was where St Peter, chosen by Jesus to be the 'rock' upon which the Church was to be built, was martyred. Alexandria had also become an important Christian centre as the result of various influential figures – including Arius – residing there.

By tradition, St Peter was considered to be the first bishop of Rome and, despite the precarious status of Christianity within the Empire, Rome became well established as the centre of Christianity in the West. Although there was no formal structure, the bishop of Rome was considered 'first among equals' by the western bishops and, over time, this authority crystallized into what we now recognize as the papacy. This was anything but immediate, however. The first use of the term Pontifex Maximus, a title used by the pope, was around AD 217. Far from being an honorific, the term was intended to imply disapproval that any Church official would be sufficiently pretentious to try to exercise their authority over others.

Nevertheless, the office of Pontifex Maximus became the central authority of the

BELOW: Created around 1365, this painting by Lippo Vanni depicts St Peter in the vestments of his office as the first bishop of Rome and therefore the first pope.

Church and early bishops of Rome were recognized as having been popes even if they never held the title. Hard facts about these individuals are scarce in some cases, but the official history of the Catholic Church names St Peter as the first pope, followed by a series of bishops of Rome who established some of the key practices of the Church. A letter attributed to St Clement, the fourth pope, was sent around AD 100 to the people of Corinth. In it, the writer objected to the removal of Church officials from office without due cause and urged the Corinthians to obey their bishops. Clement's successor, St Evaristus, is credited with the creation of parishes within Rome.

During this period, succession was not always clear and at times there might be more than one claimant to the office of Pontifex Maximus. These rival would-be popes were not at the time referred to as antipopes, but later usage of the term is appropriate. An antipope was not an enemy of the Church or of Christianity, but simply a claimant to the office other than the individual correctly elected to it.

Anyone could claim to be pope, of course, but to be recognized as an antipope the individual must have a significant following and a reasonable claim to the office. At some points in history, the question of who was pope and who was antipope would become unclear, often depending upon political or even military power for resolution. The first recognized antipope was Hippolytus, in AD 235. His antipapacy began as opposition to the legitimately elected Calixtus I, but ended in reconciliation with Calixtus's successor Pontian. It was

BELOW: The early bishops of Rome were responsible for setting out many of the practices used by the later Church. St Clement defended the authority of the Church by opposing the removal of officials by secular authorities.

this sort of internal division that the First Council of Nicaea was intended to address.

The bishop of Rome was in a precarious position before the adoption of religious freedom in AD 313. Several bishops were exiled or killed until Emperor Constantine issued his Edict of Milan, guaranteeing freedom from persecution. After this the position became a little less dangerous, although the inevitable involvement of Church officials in secular politics could create a whole range of new hazards. Emperor Honorius, ruling over a troubled and declining Western Roman Empire in the early 400s, saw the benefit of having a pope under his control. Thus Eulalius was installed as antipope against Boniface I. Divisions between Eulalius and the emperor left the antipope without support and he was soon driven from Rome.

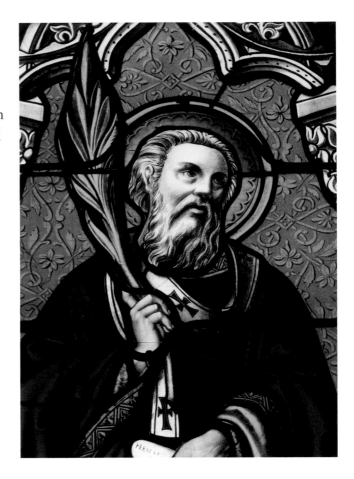

ABOVE: St Hippolytus opposed the practice of granting absolution for serious sins, and challenged some of Pope Calixtus' beliefs. During his period as antipope he was imprisoned alongside Pope Pontian during a period of persecution by Roman officials.

## CHANGING INFLUENCES

The conquest of Italy by the Ostrogothic kingdom placed Rome and its bishop in the territory of the Ostrogoths under King Theodoric. This gave Theodoric and his successors the ability to influence the election of popes to such a degree that the most important attribute of a candidate was the amount of royal support he could count on. This situation existed from 493 until 537, when Byzantine forces temporarily reclaimed the Western Roman Empire.

Although Rome was now in the territory of a different overlord, some things did not change very much. Pope Silverus, installed by the Ostrogoths, was deposed by Emperor Justinian and replaced with Vigilus. Vigilus had previously been a

VIGILIVS Rom anus, Ioannis fili= us, creatus die 27. Iunij ann.540. Sedit ann. ferè 16. Obijt an.555.

ABOVE: **Pope Vigilus involved himself in controversial issues surrounding the nature of God, Christ and the Holy Spirit. His condemnation of three writings in particular resulted in the Three Chapters Controversy, which continued long after his death.**

candidate for the office, but proved so unpopular that Pope Boniface II, who had selected Vigilus as his successor, was forced to choose another.

The Byzantine Papacy that followed the Ostrogothic Papacy saw no less interference in the selection of each new pope. The emperor had the power to approve or veto a candidate, and typically selected his preferred candidate from among Church officials he had dealings with. Thus there was a well-established route to the papacy, by way of acting as liaison to the emperor and winning his favour.

The process of obtaining approval from a distant emperor could take many months, during which the Church was essentially leaderless. However, it ensured the emperor got a pope he could rely on and demonstrated the subordination of the Church to the emperor. Thus, when Pope Martin I took office in 649 without waiting for imperial approval, the emperor was greatly displeased. Martin I was seized and taken to Constantinople to stand trial for treason. He was exiled rather than executed, a relatively merciful action that nevertheless caused problems for the Church.

Consecrating a new pope while the existing one was still alive – and had been removed from office by secular rather than religious power – was an uncomfortable proposition, but the Church had no choice. This represented renewed submission to the emperor's authority. The situation persisted until the mid-700s when Byzantium lost control of Italy to the Lombards and later the Franks. During this Frankish Papacy gifts of territory were made to the pope, which established the Papal States in Italy.

Known as the Donation of Pepin after the Frankish king Pepin (or Pippin) the Short who instigated it, this gift of land made the pope a political leader as well as a religious one. The gifted lands were former Byzantine territory, captured by the Lombards and then taken by the Franks. Naturally, the papacy was well disposed towards the new Carolingian dynasty. Further territories were gifted by Pepin's son Charlemagne, who was crowned as the first Holy Roman Emperor by Pope Leo III in 800.

THE EMPEROR HAD THE POWER TO APPROVE OR VETO A CANDIDATE, AND TYPICALLY SELECTED HIS PREFERRED CANDIDATE FROM AMONG CHURCH OFFICIALS.

## THE SPREAD OF CHRISTIANITY

Christianity had reached most corners of Europe during Roman times, often in a haphazard manner that relied on the efforts of a few individuals. The faith continued to spread after the

LEFT: The coronation of Charlemagne on Christmas Day 800 effectively created the Holy Roman Empire, though that term was not used at the time. Charlemagne assumed the role of political and military protector of the Church.

collapse of the Roman Empire, driven by two separate factors. The first was an earnest desire of those who had embraced Christianity to share it with others, with some individuals undertaking quite extraordinary journeys to convert the people of far-off lands. At the same time, politics also played a part. Rulers who were already well established with the Church found it beneficial in dealings with those who were newly converted, and religion created a measure of common ground against outsiders.

The promise of power was a strong motivator for leaders to join the new faith. From Roman times onwards, rulers and generals had taken victory over their enemies as a sign they should convert, or offered to do so if their new God would bring them success in battle. Leaders were targeted by missionaries in many cases, although some simply wandered the land preaching to anyone who would listen. However, converting a ruler was desirable since their subjects would – hopefully – follow their example or their orders and also convert.

ABOVE: St Denis was one of seven bishops sent to convert the people of Gaul by Roman Emperor Decius. He was martyred there by beheading.

## MISSIONARIES VS MONSTERS

ON MANY OCCASIONS, the local populace turned to missionaries to protect them against wild beasts that were killing livestock or ravaging the countryside. In some cases, the missionary performed miracles or confronted the monster and lectured it on the error of its ways. Others were more direct in their approach.

St Fillan was asked by the people of the Glen Dochart region to preserve them from a great boar, so he set out to hunt it. After three days he found the terrifying beast and bashed its head in with a club. The strength to do so came from his prayers, as presumably did immunity from the boar's immense tusks. Although rather mundane as miracles go, getting rid of the boar was extremely valuable to the local population and a factor in their conversion. So it was with many early saints and missionaries, who proved their worth in a rather direct manner.

The zeal of these early missionaries would make them persuasive, although it is reasonable to assume that their powers of oratory varied considerably. For every inspired preacher who could hold the attention of an entire town, there was at least one excited buffoon whose words made little sense to those who heard them. But oratory was not the only tool at the disposal of the missionaries; conversion was aided by demonstrations of power or assistance rendered to the local community.

Indeed, there was an element of bargaining involved in many of these early conversions. Whether leaders seeking victory or peasants hoping to be cured of an illness, many of those who heard the words of the missionaries wanted to know what God could do for them.

Some missionaries demonstrated the power of their faith over others by destroying objects or places sacred to pagan religions. This was a risky strategy, but one that could pay dividends. In other cases, a religious figure's place of abode could become the subject of pilgrimages and insinuate itself into the local culture. For example, St Ninian set up a ministry in Galloway at Whithorn, becoming its first bishop and creating what would become an important monastic centre.

The whitewashed stone church was certainly impressive for the time and as a religious centre it became the object of pilgrimages. Those who completed their pilgrimage were rewarded with a badge, and often criminals were given the chance to avoid punishment if they went to Whithorn and returned with a token. Some undoubtedly resorted to unsavoury means to get their badge, perhaps by stealth, deceit or murder,

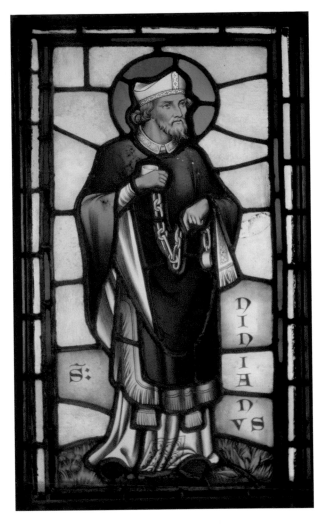

ABOVE: St Ninian is the subject of conflicting accounts that credit him with beginning the conversion of the Picts. This seems unlikely, but it is known that he was the first bishop of Galloway.

OPPOSITE: St Aristobulus is said to have been a companion of St Paul on his travels before making his way to Britain. He is credited with being the first to bring Christianity to the British Isles.

BELOW: St Patrick was captured by Irish raiders and forced to work as a shepherd. Spending long periods alone and under threat, he found strength in his faith and resolved to bring it to others.

but many did complete the task. How fervent any of these enforced pilgrims might have been is open to conjecture, but pilgrimages of this sort helped establish the early religious centres and ensured they had regular contact with people beyond their immediate region.

## THE CELTIC CHURCH

The earliest missionaries into a region did not always become its patron saints. Indeed, most will have gone unrecognized by the wider Church, contributing to the spread of Christianity at what would today be referred to as a grass-roots level. Others are a little better known. St Aristobulus is credited with introducing the faith into the British Isles in the first century by way of Spain. He is noted as the first bishop of Britain, but was eclipsed by later missionaries.

Although Christianity was established in mainland Britain during Roman times, the Church came to have a different flavour in Britain. This was largely due to Irish influences. The Celtic people of western mainland Britain and Ireland were less Romanized than those of the continent, and as a result their interpretation of Christian belief was different. The conversion of Ireland is traditionally attributed to St Patrick, although it seems likely that there were many other less famous missionaries before and after him.

According to tradition, St Patrick was captured by Irish raiders and taken from his home in England, spending several years as a captive worker. His father was a Christian deacon, but his was a mostly political role and there is no reason to suppose St Patrick was particularly zealous in his beliefs. However, during his captivity he received visions telling him to escape and return as a missionary. He duly did so, after training to be a priest.

St Patrick made decisions that would define the character of the Celtic Church. Rather than

## THE CELTIC CROSS

THE INVENTION OF THE Celtic cross is credited to St Patrick, although interpretations of its meaning differ. It is possible that the Christian cross is superimposed on the circle – symbolizing the pagan sun or moon – as a sign of Christian supremacy over the old gods, or perhaps the combination of the two was intended to appeal to those who previously worshipped the sun or moon.

RIGHT: The origins of the Celtic cross are debatable. It is possible that the circle was included to support the arms of the cross and make the carving more durable.

overthrow existing practices, he incorporated them into Christian rituals. This made the new faith more palatable to many of the Irish people, although it ultimately created divisions with the orthodox Church. In the meantime, Ireland became a major centre for Christianity, sending missionaries to mainland Britain.

The conversion of the Scots and Picts began with St Ninian in around 397. St Ninian is considered to be the first saint of Scotland, but little is known about him for sure. The site he established at Whithorn in Galloway still exists, but he is far less widely known than St Columba, who moved from Ireland to Iona and set up a monastery there. From Iona, Columba journeyed to Scotland and Ireland, converting the king (and thus the people) of Dalriada and beginning the mass conversion of what would become Scotland.

THERE WAS NO DISTINCT 'CELTIC CHURCH' AS SUCH; CELTIC CHRISTIANS WERE CHRISTIANS LIKE ANY OTHERS AND WERE PART OF THE SAME CHURCH.

Just as Arianism and Trinitarianism had been sources of contention, friction was inevitable between Celtic and orthodox

Christians. There was no distinct 'Celtic Church' as such; Celtic Christians were Christians like any others, in their own eyes at least, and were a part of the same Church. The north of mainland Britain, including Northumbria, generally followed Celtic practices, although there were many who urged compliance with the mainstream Church. Meanwhile, the rest of the country was becoming increasingly Christianized in the Roman fashion – largely due to the influence of St Augustine, first archbishop of Canterbury.

In the hope of resolving these differences, King Oswiu of Northumbria called the Synod of Whitby in 664. The abbess at Whitby was St Hilda, a relative of the king and a strong

BELOW: **Ninian's Cave at Whithorn in Galloway is believed to have been used by the saint as a retreat and a place of prayer. It has drawn pilgrims ever since, some of whom carved crosses or dates into nearby rocks.**

proponent of the Celtic Church. Despite this, the synod decided to follow Roman practices thereafter, aligning the English Church with the mainstream of Christianity. This may have been for political reasons as much as religious ones, although King Oswiu did state that as St Peter was the founder of the Roman Church and also the holder of the keys to heaven, it would be unwise to deny him.

IT IS NOT CLEAR HOW THE EARLY IRISH MONASTERIES WERE GOVERNED, BUT A PATTERN FOR MONASTIC LIFE WAS LAID OUT BY ST BENEDICT AROUND 535.

Among the matters resolved at Whitby was when to celebrate Easter. Roman and Celtic practices produced different dates, which could cause confusion and might undermine the credibility of Christianity as a whole. A more uniform set of practices was likely to impress outsiders a lot more than confusion and disorganization. In addition, the outcome of the Synod of Whitby ensured that the Celtic Church remained a local variation and did not spread to other regions. Had the synod reached a different decision, notables like the Venerable Bede might have written their histories with a more pro-Celtic slant and the Celtic Church might even have expanded into other parts of Europe.

BELOW: According to legend, St Hilda dealt with a plague of snakes by turning them to stone. Their fossilized remains can be seen below the cliffs at Whitby.

## MONASTERIES AND ABBEYS

The idea of withdrawing from mundane life to pursue a career of prayer, fasting and religious observances probably predates Christianity. Jesus fasted in the wilderness before beginning his ministry and there are accounts of holy men living apart from normal society throughout history. At some point, the idea of a shared religious life took hold; there are records of what might be considered primitive monasteries dating back to 320. The idea of a monastic existence took hold in Ireland, with communities growing up into major centres for

learning as well as religion. It was from these Irish monasteries
that the first missionaries crossed into Scotland. The community
established on Iona came to be considered the centre of Scottish
Christianity, with even bishops deferring to its authority.

A religious community of this sort had to be organized, with
strict rules governing all aspects of life. Without them, a religious
community was essentially just another village. It is not clear
how these early Irish monasteries were governed, but a pattern
for monastic life was laid out by St Benedict around 535 that
drew upon the practices and experience of earlier communities.

Not all monasteries followed the Benedictine pattern,
especially at first, but it became increasingly prevalent over time.
This owed much to Charlemagne, who supported the concept
and ensured the Rule of Saint Benedict was spread as widely as
possible. This was quite a lengthy document that outlined the
way a monastery should be run and how monks should behave.

ABOVE: **St Benedict laid
down a set of rules for
the conduct of an abbey,
which became standard
throughout Europe.
Although strict, the life
of a Benedictine monk
was much easier than
in regions where it was
believed holy men were
required to suffer daily.**

RIGHT: **The Rule of St Benedict laid out the duties of the monks, including mundane work as well as prayer and the copying of manuscripts. Among them were additional copies of the Rule, to be used by new monasteries.**

Monastic life revolved around prayer and work, with services to be held at specific times of the day and night. Much of the monks' work was mundane as the community had to support itself by farming and to maintain its buildings. Manuscripts also had to be laboriously copied and illustrated, as this was the only way to keep records or produce books. Monasteries were thus places of industry as well as prayer and at times became very wealthy through trade or the production of items such as beer, cheese and spun wool.

LIFE IN A MONASTERY WAS HARD, BUT THE MONKS (OR NUNS) WERE MUCH BETTER OFF THAN THE TYPICAL PEASANT FARMER OF THE ERA.

The monasteries became part of the political landscape all across Europe. As the Christian faith took hold, rulers became increasingly concerned about their entry into heaven. One answer to that problem was to give financial support to a monastery on the understanding that its monks would offer regular prayers for the soul of their patron. Monasteries were also places of retirement for members of noble families who either wanted to leave political life or were forced to by their enemies. Life in a monastery was hard, but the monks (or nuns) were much better off than the typical peasant farmer of the era. A sidelined nobleman might not be treated any differently to the other brothers, but a widow of a king might find retirement to a nunnery very comfortable.

It is mainly through the monasteries that records of the period survive. Literacy was rare outside the religious community and few would have the time to write a chronicle. The chances of a document surviving were much greater if it were stored in the library of a monastery than among the possessions of a private individual. Thus it is through the writings of religious figures that we see the 'Dark Ages' period and their viewpoint is often less than impartial.

Gildas, writing in around 510, blamed the invasion of Britain by Saxons and other Germanic tribes on sin and religious laxity. He recorded events to illustrate the points he was making rather than for the sake of history and is extremely vague in places. The Venerable Bede, writing in 731, was primarily concerned with the differences between Celtic and mainstream Christian practices. Thus religious sources tend to contain patchy, incomplete or highly biased information about wider events.

## A LIFE OF SUFFERING?

SOME MONASTIC CULTURES DREW on the traditions of the lone hermit, often living a life of great deprivation and suffering far from the comforts of civilization. Desert caves or deep forests were home to many hermits and some early religious communities, and some religious orders built their communities in lonely and inaccessible places. This was particularly true of the early Irish monasteries. Those communities that followed the system laid out by St Benedict were less harsh, though still subject to very strict rules.

ABOVE: Hermits lived apart from the rest of society, but not exclusively or permanently alone. Here the hermit Prudentius of Armenia visits another hermit, St Saturius of Soria.

BELOW: Monasteries were established in remote locations such as islands and peninsulas to isolate them from mundane politics. Unfortunately, this also placed them beyond the reach of assistance when Norse raiders began preying on their riches.

Monasteries were often built on good, rich land that could easily support a community, or in remote areas that set them apart from the affairs of ordinary mortals. This had some unfortunate consequences when the Norsemen began to raid European shores. Monasteries like Lindisfarne, located on an island off the Northumbrian coast, were wealthy and poorly defended. Their remote location made it extremely unlikely that help could arrive in time and in many cases the survivors were forced to abandon the site. Other sites were raided on a fairly regular basis but managed to recover sufficiently each time to become a tempting target once again.

These Norse raids have been portrayed as a war against God fought by pagan barbarians, but in reality it was simple

LEFT: **This sculpture depicts the procession of St Cuthbert's coffin around northeast England. It is likely that the coffin-bearers became a sort of mobile shrine, receiving hospitality from the villages and towns they passed through.**

opportunism. Whatever the reason, sites like Lindisfarne – the burial place of St Cuthbert – became untenable. It would be unthinkable to leave a saint behind, so the monks of Lindisfarne carried the body of St Cuthbert while they looked for a new place to settle. Eventually, after the Norman Conquest, they built a new community at Durham that became a major cathedral.

## THE BYZANTINE CHURCH

The Roman Church became the dominant form of Christianity in western Europe, eventually smoothing out discrepancies caused by local practices. The Celtic Church in the British Isles took longer to overlay, largely due to its prevalence, and did add some of its flavour to local Christian practices. However, there were significant differences between the Roman way of worship and that of the Eastern Church centred upon Byzantium.

What would become the Byzantine (or Greek Orthodox) Church had the same origins as Roman Christianity but was subject to different influences as it developed. Byzantium was closer to the origin point of Christianity than Rome and it retained many influences from its Jewish heritage. These were combined with the Greek taste for drama to create a different style of Christianity. The divergence between the two began in earnest after the Edict of Milan in 313, which permitted religious freedom in the Roman Empire, and continued as the remnants of the empire went their separate ways.

The practices used by the Byzantine Church were known as the Byzantine Rite and were formalized in Constantinople after developing in Antioch. Services were originally performed in Greek, but over time translation into local languages became permissible. The system for determining the date of religious feast days was different to that of the Roman Church and some of the rites surrounding them also differed. Byzantine Christians fasted before Christmas, much as before Easter, and performed key rites differently.

> BYZANTIUM WAS CLOSER TO THE ORIGIN POINT OF CHRISTIANITY THAN ROME AND IT RETAINED MANY INFLUENCES FROM ITS JEWISH HERITAGE.

Despite these differences, the Greek and Roman Churches remained in communion until 1054. Although different, each recognized the other as valid and sharing the same essential core beliefs. However, by the early 1050s the Roman Church was attempting to stamp its authority on communities following Greek practices in Italy and was pushing for acceptance of the pope as the supreme authority over both Greek and Roman Christians.

In 1054 a delegation from the pope arrived in Constantinople with the joint tasks of asking for help against Norman invaders pushing into Italy and convincing the Byzantine Church to subordinate itself to the pope's authority. This was an unfortunate combination of request and demand, and was rejected. The result was an exchange of excommunications between the papal legate and his Byzantine hosts.

OPPOSITE: The Edict of Milan, issued in 313, granted freedom of religion to all Roman citizens. Similar declarations had been issued before, but this one was made by a stable empire that was in a position to enforce it, and so became permanent.

This incident is known as the Great Schism, or the East–West Schism, and divided the two halves of the Church for ever after. There were many other differences, some of which were important enough to cause discord and fiery rhetorical attacks, such as whether it was acceptable to use leavened bread in the Communion rite, and after the Great Schism there was no longer any point in trying to resolve these issues.

By the time of the Crusades, the Roman Christian armies of western Europe do not appear to have considered the Byzantines as fellow Christians; the same harsh treatment was meted out to Greek Orthodox Christians as to Jews and Muslims. Had the

RIGHT: An attempt by Pope Leo IX to increase his control over the Eastern Church had the opposite effect. The ensuing Great Schism created a permanent divide between the Roman and Eastern Churches.

# GREEK OR EASTERN ORTHODOX CHURCHES?

THE TERM 'GREEK' CAME to apply to Byzantium, which had a significant population of Greek extraction and a very Greek character about its culture. Over time, some of the Eastern Orthodox Churches chose to dissociate their identity from Byzantium and dropped the term 'Greek' from their names. However, during the first millennium, the term 'Greek Orthodox' could be generally applied to any or all of the Eastern Orthodox Churches.

Great Schism not occurred, the political and military situation might have been quite different. Indeed, the final fall of the Byzantine Empire in 1453 might not have occurred – or, at least, not in the same manner – if Byzantium had remained bound to western Europe by a common Church.

## THE RISE OF ISLAM

Islam spread rapidly from its founding in Mecca and Medina in 610, creating a political entity as well as a dominant religion. Early expansion was led by the Rashidun Caliphate, with its capital initially at Medina. From 632, Rashidun forces conquered the Arabian Peninsula, pushing north as far as the Transcaucasus, and expanded along the coastal strip of North Africa as far as Tunisia.

Internal differences resulted in a period of civil war from 656 to 661, out of which a new leadership emerged. This was the Umayyad Caliphate, which further expanded the realm of Islam, notably into the Iberian Peninsula. Conflict with the Byzantine Empire was inevitable, but this was mostly along political rather than religious lines. With the new Umayyad capital at Damascus, close to Byzantine territory, a war for domination of the Middle East was inevitable. The result, however, was stalemate. Expansion north into the Caucasus met with stern resistance from the semi-nomadic Khazars. These tribal people had been encouraged by Byzantium to fight against the Sassanid Empire in Persia; after the fall of the Sassanids to the Umayyads, the Khazars continued in the same manner against their new neighbours. By doing so they protected the flank of the Byzantine Empire from Islamic expansion.

The Umayyads were more successful in Iberia. After making a series of raids on the southern shores of the Visigothic kingdom in Iberia, a force landed in 711 with the intention of conquest. It was met by a Visigothic force under King Roderic at the Battle of Guadalte, resulting in a heavy defeat for the Visigoths. Contemporary accounts of the battle are contradictory and generally unreliable, giving ludicrously inflated figures for the forces on each side. It does seem clear that the Visigoths were unable to cope with the highly mobile tactics of the Muslim cavalry and were massacred after they broke in rout.

This left the way to Toledo open. The Visigothic capital was captured while its defenders were leaderless due to the death of their king, and many other cities quickly fell or surrendered to fast-moving cavalry forces. The collapse of the Visigothic kingdom did not cause enormous disruption for the local populations. In many cases, towns that surrendered experienced little more than a change of governance; no new Islamic laws were imposed on the populace and there was no forced conversion. This may have been a wise gambit to

BELOW: The battle of Djamal, fought near Basra in 656, became popularly known as the Battle of the Camel.

LEFT: The Visigothic defeat at Guadalte in 711 has sometimes been attributed to treachery or political divisions within their force, but it is just as likely that the Visigoths were outfought by the highly mobile Muslim cavalry.

ensure the conquest of Iberia was accomplished with as little resistance as possible; it certainly had that effect.

By 717 most of Iberia was under the control of the Umayyad Caliphate and forces were beginning to push through the Pyrenees towards Toulouse. These efforts were hampered by revolts among the newly conquered Berbers, who provided much of the Muslim army's light cavalry. Expansion continued until 732, when a Muslim army under Abd-ar-Rahman was defeated near Tours by Charles Martel and an army of Franks.

THE VISIGOTHS WERE UNABLE TO COPE WITH THE HIGHLY MOBILE TACTICS OF THE MUSLIM CAVALRY AND WERE MASSACRED AFTER THEY BROKE IN ROUT.

This was a turning point in European history; the moment when the Franks began to emerge as the dominant power in western Europe and when the Islamic invasion was finally halted. It was not the end of conflict, of course, but the realm of Islam in Europe was confined to the region named Al-Andalus, which covered most of Iberia. Further attempts at expansion became less likely when the Umayyad dynasty was overthrown in 750, establishing the Abbasid Caliphate.

In 762 the Abbasids moved their capital to the newly founded city of Baghdad, adopting some of the cultural features of the previous Sassanid Empire. This was the beginning of what has been described as a golden age, in which the Abbasids funded artistic and scientific endeavour. The result was a leap forward in technology that would put the Caliphate at the forefront of progress.

Despite these advances, the Abbasid Caliphate lost territory between 756 and 969, eventually resulting in multiple Islamic states from Morocco and Iberia to Central Asia. Among these was the Caliphate of Cordoba founded by Abd al-Rahman, a member of the Umayyad dynasty. At the time of the Abbasid revolution, Rahman was in Damascus and barely escaped pursuit by leaping into the River Euphrates. After a long and dangerous journey, he found refuge in Ifriqiya, in northern Africa.

The respite was only temporary, however. Fearing betrayal to the Abbasids, Rahman resumed his travels westwards, finally landing In Iberia. There, he was able to garner support – not least due to internal divisions within the Caliphate's power structures – and to challenge the new Abbasid governors. With the Berbers in revolt and Al-Andalus in chaos, Rahman was able to capture Malaga and Seville. His enemies withdrew to Toledo while Rahman captured Cordoba, and soon afterward the Abbasid administration was swept away in a wave of support for

ABOVE: An 1862 depiction of Abd al-Rahman at the head of his army. The mobile and aggressive Umayyad style of warfare forced the Franks to create a well-trained army instead of relying upon warriors serving as and when needed.

al-Rahman, who founded a breakaway Umayyad Caliphate in Iberia. With his capital at Cordoba, Rahman made his realm a haven for those dispossessed by or fearful of the new caliphate. His strength grew to the point where his forces were able – though barely – to resist an Abbasid attempt to reassert control over Al-Andalus. From this point on, he ruled an independent Muslim state covering much of Iberia, but faced many challenges. Some were internal – rebellions or cities that chose not to accept Rahman's rule. Others came from over the Pyrenees.

Invited by the city of Zaragoza, which wanted to remain independent of Rahman's caliphate, the Frankish king Charlemagne sent an army into Iberia. The Franks were forced to retreat when Zaragoza decided it did not want to be a Frankish possession either and closed its gates. The rearguard action fought by Charlemagne's army at Roncevaux Pass became legendary and was immortalized in the epic poem *The Song of Roland*.

Zaragoza was the last major obstacle to Rahman's domination of Al-Andalus. Initially by bribery and then by force, he gained control of the city in 783. A programme of construction and road-building increased prosperity, which was an incentive for the population to accept Rahman's rule. A network of informants and messengers enabled his forces to respond to trouble in a timely manner, also increasing stability. The result was a firmly established Umayyad Caliphate in Al-Andalus that would last until 1031.

BELOW: The heroic sacrifice of Roland and his knights at the Battle of Roncevaux Pass in 778 helped establish the ideal of the 'paladin', or perfect Christian knight. It is likely that the term is a corruption of 'palatine', meaning a senior leader rather than a near-saint.

# THE MATTER OF FRANCE

JUST AS ENGLAND AND Scotland had their own bodies of classic literature (known as the Matter of England and the Matter of Scotland respectively), the legendary history of France is compiled into a collection of epic poems and chronicles known as the Carolingian Cycle, or the Matter of France.

At the heart of this literature is *The Song of Roland*, the French equivalent of the English legends of King Arthur. Blending history and romantic invention, *The Song of Roland* tells of the valiant stand by a band of heroes covering the retreat of the Frankish army. The sacrifice and heroic deaths of Roland and his companions became an ideal of knighthood as the concept of chivalry began to flower.

All of Iberia would eventually be reclaimed by Christian states, but not until the end of the 1400s.

Among the great works undertaken by the Emirate of Cordoba was a mosque built on the site of the Visigothic basilica. This used elements of Romano-Gothic design as well as concepts from Syria and the rest of the Islamic world. The city itself became a centre for learning and trade, playing an important part in the economy and politics of the western Mediterranean. Relations with the Christians over the Pyrenees remained uneasy and conflict with the Christian state in northern Spain was not uncommon, but by 800 the Emirate of Cordoba was a place of progress and civilization where ideas passed back and forth between the Christian and Islamic worlds.

LEFT: The cathedral-mosque at Cordoba started as a Visigothic church and was rebuilt as a mosque, then expanded repeatedly. It returned to Christian ownership in the early 1200s, gaining features of a Western cathedral.

# 5

# THE NORSEMEN

Often incorrectly referred to as Vikings, the Norsemen have been portrayed as bloodthirsty sea raiders who pillaged the coasts of Europe. There is some truth in that, but they were more than mere raiders. The Norsemen were also traders, settlers and conquerors, and stand among the greatest explorers of any era.

THE TERM 'NORSEMEN' is generally applied to the people of what are now Denmark, Norway and Sweden. They were not a unified kingdom for most of their history, but shared a common language and culture that permitted co-operation when it seemed desirable. This flexibility was one of the major factors of Norse society. A man might choose to join a raiding expedition one year, go trading the next and spend other years at home tending his farmstead. More than anything else, the Norsemen were opportunists – without easy, rich targets there would have been far fewer Norse raids and far more trading expeditions.

The Norsemen were a Germanic people and there is evidence they were closely related to the earliest humans to enter Europe.

OPPOSITE: This medieval depiction of Norse ships arriving in Britain is less anachronistic than many, largely because it was created closer to the era in which the Norse raiders operated. Warriors are equipped with Norman-style shields rather than their characteristic round shields.

ABOVE: **Ismantorp is an Iron Age ring fort constructed on the island of Oland around AD 200 and used for the next four centuries before being abandoned for a time. It appears to have been reoccupied around AD 900–1200.**

If so, it seems likely that they pushed north as the ice sheets retreated at the end of the last Ice Age. Settling along rivers, on the coasts and on the fringes of fjords, it was inevitable that coastal vessels would become an essential part of Norse culture. Boats and small ships carried trade goods and war parties, and it was these expeditions that gave the Norsemen their nickname of Vikings. Various theories exist regarding the origin of this term. It has been suggested that it is derived from an early Scandinavian word for pirate or that a 'Vik' was an expedition. Vikings were thus those engaged in a raiding or trading expedition,

but only until it ended. The rest of the time they were Norsemen with normal occupations such as farming or smithing.

## NORSE TECHNOLOGY AND WARFARE

The Iron Age began in Scandinavia in around 500 BC, ushering in a great leap forward in productivity. Iron ore was readily available, whereas the components of bronze had to be imported. As a result, iron weapons, armour and tools could be easily produced. This had important implications for farming, among other industries. An iron-bladed plough could turn over heavier and more fertile soil than a wooden one and allowed expansion into land that was previously too difficult to work.

Weaponry and personal protection were also subject to great advances. The typical Norseman might be armed with spear and shield if he expected a fight. Bows, javelins and hand axes were also widely available, though often as tools of the hunt and the farm rather than specifically as weapons. Those who could afford them would have fighting axes and perhaps swords.

The 'Viking' sword was of a design that became common throughout Europe. It was designed for cutting rather than thrusting, with little hand protection and a hilt that did not readily allow for use in both hands. The sword or hand axe was intended to be used in conjunction with a shield during individual combat; the spear was the primary battlefield weapon.

LEFT: The 'Viking sword' followed a pattern used, with some variations, all across Europe for several centuries. Sometimes portrayed as heavy and clumsy implements, these weapons were in fact relatively light and generally well balanced.

BELOW: A spearhead required less metal and was easier to make than a sword, but remained an effective battlefield weapon. Many spearheads were sharp enough along the edges to allow slashing cuts as well as thrusts.

Most Norse warriors were not professional fighting men. A powerful individual might be able to support a handful of well-armed followers, but the vast majority of any given force was made up of ordinary farmers equipped with whatever personal weapons they had available. Given the nature of society, this meant that a force of spearmen – some of whom would also have bows or javelins – could be quickly assembled and some of its members would have combat experience. An average Norseman would probably not have personal protection other than his shield and thick clothing, unless he inherited a piece of armour or took it as booty. More prosperous individuals might have a helmet and possibly mail armour.

Norse mail was made by 'riving' a piece of iron through increasingly small holes until it became wire, then, with the wire, creating small rings that were joined together. A full mail coat was heavy and extremely expensive; some warriors had a smaller piece of mail covering only the shoulders and upper arms. However, with the body covered by a shield and a sturdy helmet, this provided a good level of protection for the cost.

The Norse helmet was typically of a simple design with a reinforced rim and a nasal bar to protect the face. Its construction used metal strips as a framework and curved plates for the body of the helm. Known today as a Spangenhelm, this method of construction became prevalent across much of Europe. Variations did exist such as face plates, attached mail to protect the neck, and spectacle-like eyepieces, but the majority of helms were plain and functional. The 'horned helmet' associated with Vikings

LEFT: A Norse helmet from
the seventh century, found
in a boat grave at Vendel
in Sweden. Various designs
existed with eye and face
protection, but there is no
archaeological evidence
for the stereotypical
'horned helmet'.

almost certainly never existed – apart from anything else, it would be a liability aboard a ship.

Norse ships were built without an internal frame. Instead, overlapping planks were used, each nailed to the next outward from the keel. Crossbeams provided structural strength and acted as benches for rowers, with a single mast supported by a lengthways beam attached to the keel. This method was suitable for creating fast raiding vessels and larger trade ships. Initially, Norse ships were confined to coastal waters, but refinement of the technology and improvements in navigation permitted open-water voyages across the North Sea and ultimately the Atlantic Ocean.

## DRAGON SHIPS?

NORSE VESSELS ARE SOMETIMES referred to as 'dragon ships' or Drakkars. The origins of this term are obscure and do not appear to have originated with the Norsemen themselves. It may be a reference to serpentine creatures carved on the prow of some vessels or a nickname applied by a frightened raid victim. The largest Norse raiding and war vessel designs were known as Busse and Skeid, with the smaller Snekkja being more common. The Karvi was a narrower and usually smaller vessel than a Snekkja, suitable for scouting and small-scale raids.

# THE NORSE SHIELD

NORSEMEN USED A ROUND wooden shield with a central metal boss and rim. The face of the shield was made from several planks covered in leather, which was decorated by the owner if it pleased him to do so. Shields were light enough not to impede mobility and not so large that they got in the way when moving in and out of a ship. Even so, carrying the shields or several warriors aboard a small long ship presented a problem. This was ingeniously solved by fixing shields to the gunwales, providing a measure of weather protection for the rowers – they had little else – and perhaps stopping arrows in a sea fight.

A shield could be simply held up to block blows and arrows or it could be overlapped with those of other warriors to create a defensive wall, but for individual combat the lightness of the shield was a major asset. The shield was not merely a defensive obstacle; it could deflect an enemy's blow so that he was wide open for a return stroke, impede his vision of what the user's weapon hand was doing or even be used as a weapon. A thrusting blow with the rim of a shield into the face might not debilitate an opponent but it could stagger him, creating an opening for the axe or sword.

ABOVE: A depiction from c. 1930 of Norse ships under sail. Although basic, the sailing rig of these vessels was effective enough to allow long open-sea voyages.

Fighting aboard a long ship was a matter of bringing the vessel close to the enemy and engaging in an exchange of archery or a hand-to-hand battle little different to a fight on land. Generally, the boldest warrior in a boat would position himself at the prow and take on all comers until he was disabled or victorious. There were no ship-mounted weapons or rams; indeed, the design of a long ship was not well suited to surviving a collision with another vessel.

Ships were transportation rather than weapons, and even large trading vessels had a shallow draught. This allowed them to be run up on a beach during a raid, permitting warriors to disembark by leaping over the sides onto the beach. Shallow rivers could also be navigated, either to raid far inland or to carry trade goods.

## THE PRE-VIKING ERA

The Viking Age is considered to have begun in AD 793 with a Norse raid on Lindisfarne. Norsemen were well known in Europe long before this, however. Contact between the Germanic people of Scandinavia and the Roman Empire was minor and intermittent, largely due to the distance and generally hostile Germanic people in between. Scandinavia was less affected by the Hunnish invasion and the collapse of the Roman Empire, and did not see large-scale population movement in the manner of eastern Europe.

The period from AD 550 to 793 is known as the Vendel era, after large archaeological finds at Vendel in Sweden dating from this time. Europe had achieved a return to stability, with the Frankish kingdom beginning to emerge as the dominant power in the

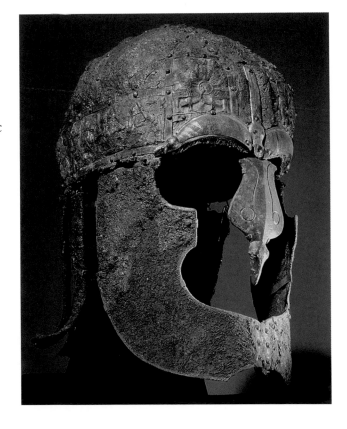

BELOW: A Vendel-era helmet from Sweden. The design of the cheek-pieces might have been influenced by Roman helmets, but sufficient experimentation was undertaken that the Vendel- era Norsemen might well have come up with the concept independently.

West. Scandinavia traded with the Franks and other European states, exporting iron and items made from it in addition to trading in goods obtained elsewhere.

COASTAL RAIDS WERE NOT NEW, BUT THE VULNERABLE RELIGIOUS SITES OF THE BRITISH ISLES OFFERED A NEW LEVEL OF PLUNDER FOR RELATIVELY LITTLE RISK.

The majority of people in Scandinavia were farmsteaders, in general individually prosperous but only loosely associated with one another. Small areas were ruled by chieftains on the basis of personal charisma, but over time the more successful leaders gained more support and wealth, which increased their influence. As chiefdoms merged and grew, large realms would eventually emerge. That day was long in the future during the Vendel period, but the more successful chieftains were extremely wealthy. Grave goods from the time include many precious items including intricate jewellery and well-crafted weapons. Notably, riding gear including stirrups was found in noble burial mounds.

Although the Norsemen on the whole preferred to fight on foot, there were exceptions and many of their leaders owned large horse herds. Contemporary writers state that the Norsemen had some of the best herds in Europe, although they did not depend upon the horse in the way that some other cultures had come to. This was not least due to the importance of maritime movement and trade.

BELOW: The Scandinavian people were capable of fine metalwork. Brooches of this type were popular in the Vendel period but were gradually replaced by oval designs.

As technology advanced and seagoing ships became a possibility, Norse traders voyaged further and became aware of the potential raiding targets along the coasts of Britain and northern Europe. Coastal raids were nothing new, but the vulnerable religious sites of the British Isles offered a new level of plunder

# WEALTH AND CURRENCY

ALTHOUGH COINS HAD BEEN issued for centuries elsewhere, the Norsemen had no coinage of their own. Currency in the ancient world was not issued on a promissory basis – it did not represent a value but was worth its weight in the precious metal it was made from. Coins were merely a convenient way of measuring out a quantity.

The Norsemen would cheerfully take and use the coinage of others, but relied on the weight of metal contained in various other objects for much of their trade. This might be decorative items; in many societies of the period, personal jewellery was essentially wearable currency. Hacksilver was also widely used. This might be cast into bars from which a quantity could be hacked off, making it convenient to carry, but lumps of silver could also be obtained by cutting up tableware and decorative items from the houses of the wealthy.

ABOVE: These coins and bracelet were made from Arabic silver, and were brought to Scandinavia by way of the river trade routes running through what is now Russia and Eastern Europe.

for relatively little risk. It was perhaps inevitable that raids would begin at some point.

## EARLY RAIDS

The first 'Viking' raid was on the monastery at Lindisfarne, in AD 793. The ferocity of the attack should not have surprised anyone; this was a violent era and coastal towns had been subjected to this sort of raiding for many years. Some towns on the southeast coast of England had been fortified since Roman times

against Saxon sea raids and defensive works had recently been undertaken in other areas.

This may have been a factor in the decision to attack the Lindisfarne monastery, which was undefended. In a Christianized Europe, raiding a holy site in this manner was simply unthinkable, but of course the pagan Norsemen had no such reservations. The attack was portrayed by the writers of the time – Christian monks – as an assault by God-hating barbarians upon the Church itself, but in truth the status of the site was of no consequence to the raiders. What they wanted was plunder, and ideally a great deal of it for little risk. Lindisfarne offered that and was thus attacked; there was no wider agenda.

The situation must have seemed quite different over the next few years, however. In 795 raiders struck the island of Iona in the Hebrides, home to another major monastery, and began attacking targets as far afield as Ireland. Religious buildings were not the only victims; anywhere that promised a good return was a potential target. That ruled out large or fortified towns as the raids of the time were on a small scale.

The usual raiding tactic was to arrive suddenly on a nearby beach, storm the target to overcome any opposition and to retreat quickly before a response could materialize. Some variation was possible, however. Rivers offered the chance to hit targets well inland, sometimes as part of a sophisticated plan whereby a raiding party would penetrate inland up a river and then march overland to the target, withdrawing by a different route to meet the ships at a prearranged point. Raiders were known to steal horses in order to facilitate greater mobility and to carry loot.

These raids increased in intensity and frequency, with some targets hit on numerous occasions. The goal was to obtain wealth

BELOW: A dramatic representation of a Norse raid at Clonmacnoise in Ireland. Any settlement within reach of the coast or a river was at risk; the most convenient were raided time and again until they were abandoned or built effective defences.

# THE ICELANDIC SAGAS

MUCH OF WHAT WE know about Norse culture and history comes from sagas written down much later. The Norsemen were not in the habit of writing records, considering history to be too important to entrust to written words. Instead, laws, histories and the deeds of heroes were memorized in the form of poems by the skalds, who recited them as needed. Using rhyme helped a skald ensure what he was saying was correct and clever phrases called kennings were used to paint a word-picture or assist in making a poem rhyme. A man might be 'the enemy of gold' if he were generous or a ship might be a 'proud sea-steed'.

These oral histories were eventually written down, notably by the Icelandic monk Snorri Sturluson. He was writing around 1200, however, and his work may have been based on partial or incorrect versions of the tales. He was also undoubtedly biased – whether or not he wanted to be – as his work had to get past the censorship of his Church superiors. Nevertheless, the sagas are the best source available for information on Norse life, culture and religious beliefs.

rather than to destroy an enemy, so on at least some occasions the amount of violence was kept to a minimum. Ideally, a settlement could be plundered but left in a state where it would be able to recover, allowing the raiders to come back in the future. Therefore, although some raids were characterized by wanton destruction and the murder of captives – and the taking of slaves for sale was common – there were occasions on which the raiders satisfied themselves with a show of force and the acceptance of tribute. As time went on, this practice grew into the Danegeld.

There was nothing wrong, to the Norseman of AD 800, with pillaging a town and killing anyone who tried to defend it. Indeed, the Norse culture held that although it was dishonourable to take property by stealth, what was won in a fight – even a grossly one-sided fight – was acceptable as booty. This attitude is illustrated by an incident from *Egil's Saga*, one

IDEALLY, A SETTLEMENT COULD BE PLUNDERED BUT LEFT IN A STATE WHERE IT WOULD BE ABLE TO RECOVER, ALLOWING THE RAIDERS TO COME BACK IN THE FUTURE.

OPPOSITE: The burning of Canterbury by Norse raiders in AD 851. Setting fire to a settlement was not just wanton destruction; it distracted the defenders.

of the Norse epic poems. Egil and his men raided a farm and found the inhabitants sleeping, so they took what they wanted and departed for their ships. Halfway there, Egil realized that this was a dishonourable act and so he marched his men back to the farm, whose inhabitants had now woken up. Egil's warriors killed the men, drove off the women and children, and burned the buildings. This victory over ill-armed and outnumbered farmers satisfied their honour and permitted Egil's band to count the raid as a legitimate success.

## EXPANSION INTO RUSSIA

The Norse people had contact with those who lived on the far side of the Baltic Sea and could navigate the River Neva from the Gulf of Finland onto Lake Ladoga. Trading expeditions plied this route from the Vendel period onwards and, wherever the Norsemen went, a few of them settled. There were opportunities in these lands, which were home to people of Slavic origin, and over time the inhabitants became known as the Rus.

Exactly how this came to pass remains open to debate. Some sources claim that cities in what is now Russia were founded by Norsemen, but the truth of this remains unclear. It is likely that energetic and ambitious Norsemen integrated within the local Slavic society and gravitated to positions of authority. This was common in the era; the ruling class and their immediate supporters tended to be warriors. As the

BELOW: Biased and distorted as they might be, Snorri Sturluson's *Prose Edda* (pictured here) and his *Poetic Edda* provide much of what is known about the Norsemen and their way of life.

Norsemen were more warlike than the local population, they naturally fulfilled this role.

Norsemen were also enthusiastic traders and skilled artisans, whose presence increased the prosperity of the local communities. Two of these, Novgorod and Kiev, grew to particular prominence as capitals of the local region and their mingled Norse/Slavic population became generally known as the Kievan Rus. It may be that the term 'Rus' was originally applied to the Scandinavian warrior class, but eventually the people as a whole became known by that name.

Much of what we know about this region comes from the *Primary Chronicle*, which was compiled in around 1100 in Kiev from a variety of sources. According to this work, the first ruling dynasty of the Rus was founded by a Norseman named Rurik. His people are referred to in the *Primary Chronicle* as Varangians, a local name for Norsemen that was also used in Byzantium.

ABOVE: The Slavic people of what is now Russia invited Rurik and his brothers, who they called Varangians, to bring an end to the fighting between their tribes around the Lake Ladoga region.

RIGHT: **Transiting the great rivers of Eastern Europe required several portages around rapids – a laborious and occasionally dangerous business. Forts were set up at some portages to protect the route or make money off those using it.**

Rurik and his warriors were invited by the local population to deal with a rebellion by the local tribes, which was threatening trade routes and settlements in the region of Lake Ladoga.

Rurik founded a settlement named Holmgard, which according to legend grew into the city of Novgorod. After his death in 879, Rurik's brother Oleg took command and led a campaign to capture Kiev. Kiev became the capital of the Rus state; by tradition, the ruler's heir would reside in the northern capital of Novgorod with the Rus as a whole governed from Kiev. The Rurik dynasty is today considered to be the beginnings of the Russian state.

IT IS KNOWN THAT NORSEMEN HAD EXTENSIVE DEALINGS WITH THE BYZANTINE EMPIRE AND TRADED IN GOODS COMING FROM THE EAST ALONG THE SILK ROAD.

The Kievan Rus prospered in part due to their position on the trade routes of eastern Europe. From the Lake Ladoga region it was possible to access the Dnieper and Volga rivers, allowing a voyage all the way to the Black and Caspian seas. This was no easy undertaking, as it required portages at several rapids along the way. The usual method was to unload the ship and transport the cargo overland around the rapids, then pick up the ship and carry it to a deeper part of the river before reloading it and setting off again. By this laborious method, goods could be moved in bulk all the way from the Baltic to Byzantium.

It is known that Norsemen had extensive dealings with the Byzantine Empire and traded in goods coming from the east along the Silk Road. What is less clear is how far the Norsemen themselves travelled east. Given their energetic and inquisitive nature, it is probable that some journeyed over huge distances. Wild claims that Norsemen reached China or sailed their long ships out of the Yangtze estuary to lands beyond have no basis in reality, but do resurface from time to time.

## NORSEMEN IN BYZANTIUM

The Rus came into conflict with the Byzantine Empire from time to time, beginning in 860 when a large-scale raid caught Byzantium unprepared and plundered the city. It is likely that the Rus leaders were well informed about events to their south

## THE DNIEPER PORTAGES

THERE ARE SEVEN MAJOR **rapids on the Dnieper River and most have Scandinavian names. These areas may well have had local names, but it was the Norse traders who negotiated them on their voyages who would tell others about them, ensuring that their names were the ones that spread and were recorded. The trading posts and forts that were built to protect and control these portages gradually grew into major communities in their own right, generating wealth for their owners from the trade routes.**

The Dnieper is the fourth-longest river in Europe. It gave Norse mariners access to the Black Sea and trade opportunities around its shore by way of Kiev.

and knew that most of the Byzantine Army had been drawn off to fight Muslim forces. This exploit clearly demonstrated the fighting prowess of the Varangians and the fact that the Byzantine emperor preferred to have them fight for him than against him.

Byzantium thus became a source of employment for Rus and Norsemen. The best or most renowned were recruited for the Varangian Guard, part of the emperor's bodyguard, but any warrior could find work in Byzantium. Norsemen gave good service all around the Mediterranean, becoming noted for the long-handled axes they favoured as their primary weapon. So many young men went to Byzantium to seek their fortune that laws were passed that a man could not inherit while he was 'in Greece', as Byzantine service was called. This ensured that at least some of the warriors returned home after their time in the Mediterranean.

Those who did return home had been well paid during their service and were in a position to set themselves up as men of substance. The wealth they brought home fed into the Rus and Scandinavian economies but also encouraged others to seek Byzantine service. What in other eras might be considered a 'brain drain' – in this case, more of a swordarm drain – took place, but conversely many of the successful later Norse leaders learned their trade 'in Greece' and used their experience to good effect elsewhere.

The Varangian Guard outlived the Viking Age and was still fighting the enemies of the Byzantine emperor long after its parent society had morphed into something new.

BELOW: Emperor Theophilus was one of many Byzantine rulers to be protected by the Varangian Guard. Unlike the Praetorian Guard of the Western Roman Empire, the Varangians were generally aloof from local politics and thus far more reliable.

The secret of this longevity was more than simple combat prowess. The Varangians were outsiders, less likely to be drawn into the plots of the imperial court than local troops, and came from a culture where loyalty was highly prized. The Varangians were more reliable than other troops; a trait greatly valued by the Byzantine emperors. They might have been rough around the edges and drunk so much they were nicknamed the 'Emperor's Wineskins', but they could be relied upon under almost any circumstances.

## NORSE RELIGION AND CHRISTIANITY

The Norsemen had a close, almost family, relationship with their gods. Rather than being distant and frightening beings, the Norse gods were seen as being close by and – although powerful and certainly to be respected – could be railed at by someone who felt his gods had let him down. A man might direct a tirade at a god, demanding help and threatening to no longer venerate the deity if he were not successful in his endeavours.

ABOVE: A depiction of the battle of Ragnarök, in which most of the Norse gods would die saving what was left of the world from monsters and giants.

# LOYALTY

To the Norse warrior, loyalty was a two-way street. A leader made gifts to his warriors, held feasts for them and treated them with respect. In return, he could expect his men to be faithful and reliable. A ruler who slighted his warriors or took their loyalty for granted might find some or all of them deserting him for a more worthy leader. This situation changed over time, as the Norse lands became kingdoms and the organization of military forces more impersonal, but the cultural traits of forthright loyalty and mutual respect remained a part of Norse society.

ABOVE: **Odin was a complex god. A fearsome warrior and a cunning, deceitful king, he also personified wisdom and could perform magic. His eight-legged horse Sleipnir could run between worlds.**

The Norse pantheon was complex, consisting of two groups of gods – the Aesir and the Vanir – who represented war and fertility. Their enemies were the Jötnar, or Giants, who they had overthrown to become rulers of the universe. This conflict was destined to end in the great battle of Ragnarök, in which most of the gods would die. The best human warriors would spend the ages after their deaths in the halls of Valhol and Fólkvangr, feasting and preparing for the battle.

Ragnarök was to be a time of enormous destruction, with countless mortals and gods slain and even the world itself broken. Yet it was also a time of rebirth, in which the remnants of the world would be replaced by a better one and the survivors would live a life of plenty. The idea that everything, even gods, must have an ending was prevalent throughout Norse religion and philosophy. A short but notable life was better than a long and mundane one, and what mattered more than anything else was leaving others with positive memories.

The Norse gods each fulfilled a particular role within their society, but most had more than one aspect. Thus Odin, the Allfather, was a wise and cunning king but also a mystic who could perform magic. Thor was a warrior first and foremost but farmers revered him for bringing the rain.

The Norsemen were aware of Christianity through their trade links and will not have been surprised or dismayed when missionaries began arriving in their homelands. Indeed, many Norsemen were quite happy to recognize the Christian God; they had plenty already so one more was not going to cause problems. Moulds have been found by archaeologists that are suitable for casting either a Christian cross or a pagan hammer, the symbol of Thor. This suggests that those who wanted to embrace Christianity were tolerated – and proved a lucrative market for religious items – or that many Norsemen worshipped the Christian god alongside their own.

It is likely that the early missionaries were exasperated by this attitude. People were supposed to convert and renounce their old gods, not accept and absorb the new one as part of their existing pantheon. Despite what certain monastic writings may say about the conversion of the heathen Norsemen by zealous and saintly missionaries, it is likely that the spread of Christianity was patchy and not in any way what the missionaries had hoped for. Similarly, Norsemen who settled in lands containing a Christian population seem to have adopted some elements of their religion without a dramatic moment of conversion or a complete abandonment of pagan symbology.

Eventually, however, the Norse kingdoms became Christian. This was more a matter of persuading the population that Christianity was their only religion than of making them adopt it. It seems that the Norsemen did not take readily to the idea of monotheism and only became 'proper' Christians over a long period.

One reason for the conversion of rulers – which in turn led to the general populace becoming Christianized – was political. As the Norse kingdoms became more like those of Europe and became involved in international politics rather than raiding, alliances became desirable. A fellow Christian was more likely to be an acceptable partner than a pagan barbarian. The same applied at lower levels; Norse merchants were more acceptable to their foreign clients if they were civilized

BELOW: **Runestones were created before and after the coming of Christianity to Scandinavia. This one, depicting Christ, was commissioned by King Harald Bluetooth in the 960s.**

Christians, so those who embraced at least the trappings of Christianity were in general more successful in their endeavours. The Norsemen were, above all, a pragmatic and opportunist people. They would raid or trade – or stay at home and farm – depending on what offered the best return for their effort. They seem to have approached religion the same way. Just as there was nothing religious about the decision to sack monasteries – whatever Christian writers of the time might have thought – the decision to embrace Christianity may well have been equally pragmatic. The new religion offered opportunities and advantages, and was thus preferable to the old one.

NORSEMEN BRAVED THE OPEN SEAS IN SHIPS WITH VIRTUALLY NO WEATHER PROTECTION AND ONLY THE MOST RUDIMENTARY OF SAILS.

BELOW: Norse ships are often depicted with a dragon's head carving on the prow. A variety of other designs have been found, including serpents, but there is no archaeological evidence for 'dragon ships' in this sense.

## EXPLORATION

Any maritime journey was fraught with risk, even a short haul down the coast to a known location. Yet the Norsemen braved the open seas in ships with virtually no weather protection and only the most rudimentary of sails. Even on known routes, the

arrival point could be quite variable due to currents and the vagaries of the wind. A vessel crossing the North Sea headed for the Northumbrian coast might actually make landfall in East Anglia or southern Scotland. On journeys of this sort, without sophisticated navigational equipment or even good charts, the only option was to head in roughly the right direction and hope to recognize landmarks once land was sighted.

Crossing a wider body of open water was even more of a challenge. The early explorers who headed out into the Atlantic Ocean could not know for sure if there was a landfall to make. At some point, they had to decide whether to push on and hope to find land before their supplies ran out or to turn back and hope to reach a friendly shore. Undoubtedly many ships were lost this way and many of the great discoveries were largely accidental.

The Norsemen knew the British Isles existed and that they could access them easily by sailing along the north coast of Europe before turning to cross the narrow gap. Once the coast of Britain was explored, a crew on the western coast of Norway knew with reasonable certainty that they could reach Britain by heading westwards. This was not a voyage for the faint-hearted, however; the last sight of land would be a poignant moment for many early mariners.

Other regions could be explored by following the coasts; Ireland and the Isle of Man by sailing around Scotland and the entrance to the Mediterranean by following the European coastline. Norse trade ships and raiders would enter the Mediterranean and operate there for a time before making the long transit home. The ability to beach ships at night was useful,

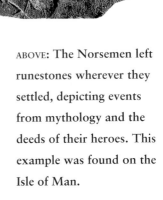

ABOVE: The Norsemen left runestones wherever they settled, depicting events from mythology and the deeds of their heroes. This example was found on the Isle of Man.

RIGHT: Some areas settled by the Norsemen have remained in use ever since. The remains of a Norse settlement dating from over a thousand years ago can be seen at Kvivik in the Faroe Islands.

but still required care – the local population might have reasons not to be well disposed towards a crew of Norsemen they found sleeping on their shores.

For those heading outward from these known shores, the horizon was entirely unknown. Yet Norse expeditions found the Faroe Islands in around AD 825 and set up colonies there. It has been suggested that the islands were already inhabited when the Norsemen arrived, perhaps settled from the Orkneys or the Shetlands. There is a reference in the work of Dicuil, an Irish monk, to islands reached by sailing north from Britain and accounts exist of how the first Norse explorers to land in Iceland found a community of Irish monks there.

Thus it is possible that the early Norse explorers had good reason to believe there was land to be found just over the horizon. However, an island group like the Faroes is a small target in a very large sea, and a ship sent off course by wind and tide might miss them entirely. This is apparently how Iceland was discovered; by sailors headed for the Faroes. As the population of the island communities grew, sea communication between them and the mainlands increased and navigational accuracy improved – though only on a rule-of-thumb basis as sailors learned the local currents and weather patterns.

It is possible that the Norsemen used naturally occurring polarizing materials to assist in navigation. Known as Sunstone, these crystals could be used to indicate the location of the sun even on a cloudy day, allowing a course to be estimated. There are mentions of such materials in the Norse sagas and some evidence that they may have been used. Certainly, the theory is sound – some animals and birds are known to be able to see the polarization of sunlight and use it for navigation.

BELOW: Iceland spar is a form of calcite that polarizes light. This may be the 'sunstone' referred to in some sagas as assisting navigation on the open seas.

## GAINING LARGE KINGDOMS

Population movement out to the islands was driven by opportunism to some extent; an individual could claim some good land before others reached the islands, and by political pressures. By the late 800s the Norse lands were coalescing into large kingdoms, which was not to the liking of everyone. Some preferred to be more independent; others sought to move away from their enemies. Thus the newly discovered lands in the Shetlands, Orkneys and Faroes had a certain appeal. Living in a group of fairly small islands was also attractive to an essentially maritime people.

The discovery of Iceland resulted in a similar population drift, with

a new wave of migrants following the explorers. According to the *Íslendingabók* (Book of the Icelanders), all the good land was taken by AD 930, although there is evidence that population migration continued well after this. In time, Iceland grew into a nation in its own right, rejecting the idea of kings in favour of a more democratic system. Iceland as a whole remained apart from the events unfolding in Europe, although individuals journeyed back and forth to seek their fortune. The normal pattern was to sail to Iceland one year and back the next, making a trade expedition no small endeavour. However, once it was known that the land was there, the intrepid Norse mariners made such crossings of the dangerous Norwegian Sea a regular occurrence.

BELOW: **The Althing, or national parliament, was held at Thingvellir from 930 to almost 1800. It was declared a national park in 1928, to protect its unique heritage and the local wildlife.**

The discovery of Greenland may have been based on the assumption that if there was land to be found sailing west from Norway, there must be more west of Iceland. This was confirmed around AD 930 when Icelandic mariners blown far to the west by a storm reported seeing land. It was not until 980 that this discovery was investigated further, however. Erik the Red, already outlawed in Norway, committed misdeeds that earned him a three-year period of outlawry in Iceland too. He chose to explore westwards until he could return safely and investigated the shores of Greenland.

At the time Erik the Red landed in Greenland, the climate was warmer than at present. Greenland was habitable, at least in sheltered areas, and Erik set up a colony there. His new homeland lacked timber for shipbuilding and a nearer source than Scandinavia or Scotland was desirable. A Norse mariner – again, blown off course, this time while heading for Greenland – had sighted land in 986. Once the Greenland colony was established, one of Erik the Red's sons, Leif Eriksson, led an expedition to investigate further.

Leif Eriksson probably first landed in the Americas on Baffin Island, which did not impress him with its natural resources. It did become a landfall during further exploration and trade with the local population was undertaken. Further expeditions found

ABOVE: **A statue of Erik Thorvaldsson, better known as Erik the Red, stands at the village of Qassiarsuk in Greenland. In Erik's day the settlement was known as Brattahlid.**

ABOVE: Leif Eriksson's crew were the first Europeans to sight the North American continent in the distance, and soon afterward became the first to set foot upon it. It is likely that they landed in Newfoundland and never visited the mainland.

the coast of Labrador, which had plenty of timber, and wintered on an island off the coast of the American continent. This was probably Newfoundland, which was inhabited by Norsemen during the winter of 1001–02.

In 1009 or 1010, Erik the Red's son-in-law Thorfinn Karlsefni led an expedition to colonize the new territory, taking over Leif Eriksson's fortified camp. He brought with him 65 followers, of whom five were women. The Norse colonization of the Americas was short-lived; the colony was abandoned after just three years, but in that time a child was born. This was Thorfinn's son Snorri, who would be the only person of European stock born in the Americas for several centuries.

The Norsemen came into conflict with the local population, whom they called Skraelings ('wretches'). They cheated the Skraelings in trade and mistreated them, confident their fortified camp and European weaponry would keep them safe from retaliation. However, with the Norse settlement in a state of siege, the colony became unviable and was abandoned.

There were no Norsemen living on the North American

continent after 1015, although it is possible that trade relations were maintained with those local tribes that had not been entirely alienated. The Greenland colony declined and, as the climate cooled, navigation of the waters off Greenland became more difficult. Advancing ice on land and frozen seas resulted in a decline and eventual collapse of the colony. There were still people of Norse extraction living in Greenland into the mid-1400s; the final date of the colony is unknown.

Thorfinn Karlsefni's colony in Newfoundland marks the westernmost point of Norse settlement, and probably of exploration too. It has been repeatedly suggested that 'Vikings' landed on the American mainland and left their mark there, but all of the evidence presented has turned out to be mistaken or a deliberate hoax. Nevertheless, the legend of Vikings in North America remains an attractive one – and given their nature, it is not quite beyond the

THE NORSE COLONIZATION OF THE AMERICAS WAS SHORT-LIVED; THE COLONY WAS ABANDONED AFTER JUST THREE YEARS, BUT IN THAT TIME A CHILD WAS BORN.

BELOW: Leif Eriksson named his discovery Vinland. The meaning of this term, and the location of Vinland, has been debated ever since.

bounds of possibility that Norsemen did indeed sail their ships up the St Lawrence River around 1000 years ago.

### NORSE POWER IN BRITAIN

Norsemen had always settled wherever they could find good land, initially on a haphazard basis. There was no large-scale migration as there had been in the case of the Saxons and similar Germanic tribes, but a general drift into new lands occurred as soon as they were discovered. Norsemen are known to have settled in the region of Dublin from AD 840 onwards, initially becoming part of the local political landscape and later emerging as a major power. Conflict was common, but there was no clear-cut 'us and them' situation in most areas. The local Norse population were one more faction in the shifting tribal politics or political situation and might find allies as readily as enemies.

The city of Novgorod is thought to have been founded by the Rus in 862, marking the beginning of the Norse kingdoms of Russia. Four years later, a Norse kingdom was founded in Jorvik (modern-day York). This came about largely due to internal troubles in Northumbria. A large Norse Army landed

## THE KENSINGTON RUNESTONE

IN 1898 A RUNE-CARVED stone was found in Kensington, Minnesota, 'proving' that Norsemen did indeed explore the region and perhaps settled there for a time. Other artefacts have also been found, but in all cases these finds have turned out to be hoaxes. There is no evidence that Norsemen settled the North American continent.

The Kensington runestone caused quite a stir when it was discovered, but linguistic discrepancies provoked an investigation that debunked the find as a hoax.

LEFT: The JORVIK museum in York (formerly known as Jorvik when under Norse rule) contains a recreation of a typical settlement. Such villages were not very different from those of the Anglo-Saxons and other people of the time.

in East Anglia in 866, the same year the Northumbrian king Osbert was overthrown and replaced by his brother Aella. After wintering in East Anglia, the Norsemen advanced into what is now Yorkshire and defeated King Aella. After putting him to death in gruesome fashion, they installed a puppet king and moved on to new conquests.

The Norse Army was referred to by contemporary writers as the Great Heathen Army. After capturing York the force marched into Mercia, causing a great deal of destruction before negotiating a withdrawal to York. Despite previously accepting tribute rather than ravaging East Anglia, the Great Heathen Army conquered the region in 869, launching further campaigns against Mercia and Wessex. The Great Heathen Army was finally defeated in 878 at the Battle of Edington by Alfred the Great of Wessex. A treaty was agreed in 886 giving control of the eastern side of England to the Norsemen. This region, stretching from the border of Northumbria to the Thames estuary, was known as the Danelaw.

> NORSEMEN HAD ALWAYS SETTLED WHEREVER THEY COULD FIND GOOD LAND, INITIALLY ON A HAPHAZARD BASIS.

## THE UNIFICATION OF NORWAY

The chiefdoms of Scandinavia gradually consolidated into a system of local small kingdoms, within which areas were

# RAGNAR LODBROK

LITTLE IS KNOWN FOR sure about the legendary Ragnar Lodbrok.

According to legend, he wore magical trousers (his 'hairy-breeks', after which he was named) to protect him from the flames of a dragon that he slew. He was captured and put to death by the Northumbrian king Aella, who was in turn killed by Ragnar's sons after the conquest of Northumbria.

BELOW: The Flateyjarbók contains a number of sagas including that of King Harald Fine-Hair, who is depicted here freeing the giant Dofri. The manuscript also includes histories of the Orkney and Faroe islanders, and of the colony in Greenland.

controlled by jarls to whom the chieftains owed allegiance. The move toward a large kingdom began with Halfdan the Black in 860. Halfdan was the son of Gudrød the Hunter and had a claim to his father's realm, but was forced to fight his half-brother Olaf for it. With his power base established, Halfdan brought other petty-kingdoms under his control by a combination of conquest and negotiation.

Halfdan was killed when his horse fell through the ice on a frozen lake around 870 or 880, leaving his son Harald as king. Harald was only 10 years old at the time, but managed to keep most of his father's gains. His subsequent conquests were undertaken, apparently, to impress a girl. Seeking to win over a princess from Hordaland, he vowed not to cut his hair until he had conquered all of Norway. He kept this promise, although he was known as Harald Mop-Hair during the 10 years the campaign took him, and married his princess. He was thereafter known as Harald Fine-Hair.

Harald's unification of Norway was not to everyone's liking. During his reign he had to deal with rebellions and raids from enemies who set up bases in remote fjords and in Scotland.

Control was consolidated after a coalition of enemies was defeated near what is now Stavanger in 890. Many of Harald's former opponents, or those who did not want to live under his rule, moved away to new lands. This increased the pace of colonization and expansion elsewhere.

After Harald's death, his son Eric took the throne. Eric's early career was spent raiding and plundering in a true 'Viking' manner, and he was not a gentle ruler. Much of what is known about Eric – who is better known by his nickname 'Bloodaxe' – comes from sagas that may be at least in part fictional. He appears to have consolidated his rule by killing his father's other children, until he was overthrown by his surviving brother Haakon.

Eric Bloodaxe resumed his career as a sea raider for a time before seeking his fortune in Northumbria. It appears he was given the throne of Northumbria by the English king Aethelstan in the hope that he would create a buffer state against the depredations of other Norsemen and the Scots. This was not entirely successful. Eric Bloodaxe was driven out of Northumbria twice, ruling there from 947 to 948 and from 952 to 954. He was eventually killed at the Battle of Stainmore in 954, bringing to an end the intermittent Norse kingdom of Northumbria.

ABOVE: Eric Haraldsson, better known as Eric Bloodaxe, was king of Norway for a time, and king of Northumberland twice. His eventful life typified the adventurous spirit of the Norsemen.

# DANES OR NORSEMEN?

MANY CONTEMPORARY WRITERS REFERRED to all Scandinavians as 'Danes'. Sometimes this was accurate, sometimes not.

The more general term 'Norsemen' also includes inhabitants of Sweden and Norway, as well as populations of Norse extraction such as at Dublin or in Iceland. 'Norsemen' can be substituted for almost any reference to 'Danes' found in contemporary writings.

# 6

# KINGDOMS OF EUROPE

The last 200 years of the 'Dark Ages' saw the emergence of powerful feudal kingdoms that would shape the fate of Europe for the next centuries. Greatest among them was the Frankish Kingdom, which would eventually create the nation of France and the Holy Roman Empire.

UPON THE death in AD 768 of Pippin III (also known as Pepin the Short), the realm of the Franks was divided among his sons, as was the custom of the time. Three years later, the death of Pippin's eldest son Carloman resulted in his younger brother Charles – better known to history as Charlemagne – becoming sole ruler of the Frankish lands.

Charles was at the time married to a Lombard princess who was probably named Geperga, creating an alliance with the Lombards of northern Italy that did not greatly please the pope. The death of Carloman placed Charles on a unified Frankish throne, but his position was tenuous. To cement his claim, he sent Geperga home and married a Frankish noblewoman instead. This created a certain amount of ill-feeling in the

OPPOSITE: **Any city on or near a river was at risk of being attacked by the Norsemen. Their attack on Paris in AD 885 was unusual in that it took the form of a siege rather than a raid.**

Lombard realm, resulting in the Lombard king Desiderius giving refuge to Carloman's widow and his young sons.

A dispute between Desiderius and the pope in around 772 gave Charlemagne a pretext to invade and conquer the lands of the Lombards. Lombardy thereafter was a Frankish possession and the Iron Crown of Lombardy became part of the regalia of the Holy Roman Empire. The foundation of that empire was still some years away at this time, however, and Charlemagne faced opposition from the west. He campaigned against the Saxons and their allies, the Frisians, extending his realm over the next 30 years.

Charlemagne was not a merciful conqueror and was particularly harsh towards pagans or those who would not accept Christianity. This might have won him the approval of the pope, but it inspired fear and hatred among his conquered peoples. Nor did all of his campaigns end well. In 778, in response to a request for assistance form the semi-independent city of Zaragoza, Charlemagne marched into Iberia. This campaign ended in defeat, not least because the city changed its mind about the desirability of Frankish overlordship. To forestall further threats from that direction, Charlemagne granted his son Louis rulership over Aquitaine, from where a series of campaigns created a Frankish foothold in what is now northern Spain.

With his southwestern frontier reasonably secure, Charlemagne turned his attention eastwards once again, annexing Bavaria and defeating the declining Avar realm. It was not possible to secure such a large empire by force alone, but

ABOVE: Pippin III followed the Frankish practice of dividing his realm up among his sons rather than keeping it intact and passing it to a sole heir. This subdivision of power weakened realms and tended to cause conflict.

Charlemagne made effective alliances. His good relationship with the pope was extremely useful, and he maintained relations with distant powers such as the Byzantine emperor and the Abbasid caliph. He also involved himself in the affairs of the English kingdoms, although his relationship with Offa of Mercia was a difficult one.

The Frankish Empire under Charlemagne was divided into counties, each ruled by a count who administered the territory and derived his income from it. The holders of these positions were, for the most part, members of aristocratic families that had supported Charlemagne and had a vested interest in continuing

BELOW: Relations between the Franks and the Lombards were soured by a dispute over previously Lombard territory given to the pope by the victorious Franks. The result was another Frankish conquest – this time at the hands of Charlemagne.

to do so. At the same time, religious officials were granted immunity from secular authority. This system was effective and endured long after the reign of Charlemagne himself.

Charlemagne's reign saw the beginnings of the feudal system that would dominate European society for the next few centuries. Officials were appointed according to royal favour and those who supported the Crown were rewarded with income or offices that allowed them to generate it. At the same time, economic measures increased prosperity. Weights and measures were standardized, and royal officials would enforce compliance. The result was a stronger and more vibrant economy, which in turn increased stability by creating an incentive to support the status quo.

In 799 Pope Leo III was assaulted by his opponents and sought refuge with Charlemagne. The Franks provided military protection and assistance to the pope, enabling him to face

# CAROLINGIAN WARRIORS

CONTEMPORARY SOURCES DESCRIBE CHARLEMAGNE and his men as being clad entirely in iron, but clear information on Carolingian war gear is hard to come by. Many depictions of Carolingians are entirely anachronistic, giving them either Roman-style equipment or armour of a sort that was not invented for another 500 years. In all probability the ordinary warriors were equipped with spear and shield, perhaps with a helmet, and had no body armour. The elite of the army wore good-quality mail hauberks reaching to mid-thigh and fought on horseback with lance and sword.

Carolingian cavalry are often depicted wearing a hauberk of scale or mail, with a metal helmet.

down his opponents and restore his primacy. This created a new concept in European politics – the military protector of the Church and enforcer of the pope's will.

## THE HOLY ROMAN EMPEROR

On Christmas Day 800, Pope Leo III crowned Charlemagne 'Emperor of the Romans'. 'Roman' in this context implied not citizens of Rome, Italy or the long-vanished empire, but the civilized inheritors of culture and learning. 'Romans' were essentially the civilized people of Europe and Charlemagne was their emperor… at least according to Pope Leo III.

This coronation gave Charlemagne the authority to act against the enemies of the pope and established him as the guardian of all Christendom. However, this did not mean the Holy Roman Empire was suddenly established all across Europe. It was two years before Charlemagne began to refer to himself as 'Emperor Governing the Roman Empire' and he seems to have continued

Paes la mort De lempereur
loys qui par sonnom fut ap
pelle loys le Debonnaire qui
fut filz charlemaigne Deux
De ses filz Lothaire et loys assemblerent
grās osts & toutes pars & le's royaulme!
côtre charles se chaustse leur frere q estoit
roy De frāce Doir est quil nestoit seur free
re que De pere car il fut filz De la Derrenies
re Dame q eut nom iudich Moult auoiet

ABOVE: Louis the Pious was not the emperor his father had been. Where Charlemagne warred against external foes and built an empire, Louis battled his sons and struggled not to lose it.

to see himself as a Frankish king rather than something larger.

The name 'Holy Roman Empire' would not be used until the 1200s, but the idea of a powerful monarch presiding over a Christian Europe was now established. After the death of Charlemagne in 814, he was succeeded by his son Louis the Pious. Louis appears to have seen himself as an emperor of the Christians, although he followed the Frankish practice of dividing his realm among his sons.

The sons of Louis the Pious proved troublesome. At times they conspired or fought against one another; eventually they allied against their father. In 833 Louis was forced to abdicate, but the following year he was restored to his position. Reconciliation followed, and in due course Louis's son Lothair was crowned co-ruler in the Frankish tradition. Lothair inherited his father's position, but subdivision was the Frankish way in that era and, despite brief reunifications, the Carolingian Empire had disintegrated by 900.

Francia remained divided by its internal politics and the schemes of its rulers, which prevented coherent action against the depredations of Norse raiders. Later Carolingian rulers lacked the energy and effectiveness of Charlemagne, resulting in a downward spiral that finally ended when the house of Capet took the throne of Francia in 987. Nevertheless, their realm – under a new line of kings – would endure throughout the medieval period and beyond.

## NORSE RAIDS IN EUROPE

With the Carolingian Empire at its height, the northern coast of Europe was relatively secure against attacks by even very

large forces of Norsemen. Charlemagne's bloody campaigns in
the east against the Saxons resulted in an appeal for help from
their northern neighbours, but it was not until after the death
of Charlemagne that large-scale Norse raids began to seriously
trouble the Frankish kingdom.

From 820 onward, large forces of Norse warriors began
sailing up the rivers of northern France, notably the Seine, to
attack major cities. The initial raid, consisting of 13 ships, was
driven off but others followed. The Frankish kingdom was
suffering from internal troubles at the time, as the sons of Louis
the Pious fought over their father's realm. As a result, a large raid
sacked Rouen in 841.

Defensive measures were put in place, such as fortifying
bridges to create river forts, but this did not prevent Paris from
coming under siege in 845. A force of 120 ships pushed up the
Seine and were met by an army under Charles the Bald. With
the two halves of the Frankish army divided by the river, the
Norsemen were able to concentrate against and defeat one
force before advancing on Paris itself. They found most of the
population had fled and, with their line of withdrawal threatened
by Charles the Bald's army, they were not in a good position. For
his part, Charles felt unable
to force a military solution
and instead bribed the
Norsemen to go away.

This was the first
example of what would
become known as
Danegeld; a ruler paying
the Norsemen to leave his
territory alone. This suited
the Norsemen themselves;
they could raid somewhere
else or collect tribute while
they saw to other affairs.
The ability to extort
Danegeld and control

BELOW: A poor defensive
strategy allowed an army
of Norsemen, traditionally
claimed to have been
led by Ragnar Lodbrok,
to lay siege to Paris. In
addition to plundering,
the Norsemen were able
to extort a huge bribe in
return for leaving.

ABOVE: Charles II (Charles the Bald) had a troubled reign beset by Norse raids, unreliable vassals and conflict with his brother Louis the German. Charles was forced to resort to bribing his enemies to cease their attacks.

their followers well enough that other realms thought it worth paying depended on changes in the nature of Norse society. The fragmented chieftaindoms and petty-kingdoms of a century earlier could not have engaged in this sort of industrial-scale extortion racket – not least because there were no leaders strong enough to stop others continuing to raid.

Another large-scale Norse incursion into the Frankish realm began in 851. Rouen was captured and used as a base for further raids, and further bribes were extorted out of the Frankish king by capturing abbeys to be held hostage rather than being plundered and destroyed. The best countermeasure to Norse raids turned out to be the Norsemen themselves; from 860 Charles the Bald paid bands of Norsemen to defend his rivers against the raids of others. This had unfortunate consequences for others; the difficulty of obtaining plunder from Francia may have been a factor in directing the Great Heathen Army towards East Anglia and ultimately the eastern half of England.

In 876 Charles the Bald paid another vast sum to get rid of a Norse fleet of 100 ships that had again captured Rouen and was causing great destruction. He died the following year and eventually the throne passed to Charles the Fat, who was more concerned with events elsewhere. Thus when another Norse army attacked Paris in 886, it fell to Count Odo to defend the city. His strategy, based on using a fortified bridge to deny access, was successful in defeating the first assault but could not prevent a siege.

Paris was eventually relieved by its king, Charles the Fat, who followed what was becoming standard practice by bribing the Norsemen to go elsewhere. He added a new twist, however. Rather than simply returning home, Charles the Fat paid his enemies to attack Burgundy. This might have been an astute piece of statecraft, setting a current enemy against a potential one, but it could not prevent Charles from being overthrown in favour of Odo.

After Odo's death, the throne passed to Charles the Simple, who inherited the problem of Norsemen becoming established in the northern coastal regions. Expelling them proved impossible,

BELOW: Count Eudes, often known as Odo – the Germanic form of his name – led a successful defence of Paris in 885– 886. He was subsequently elected king of the Franks, but his selection was not universally accepted.

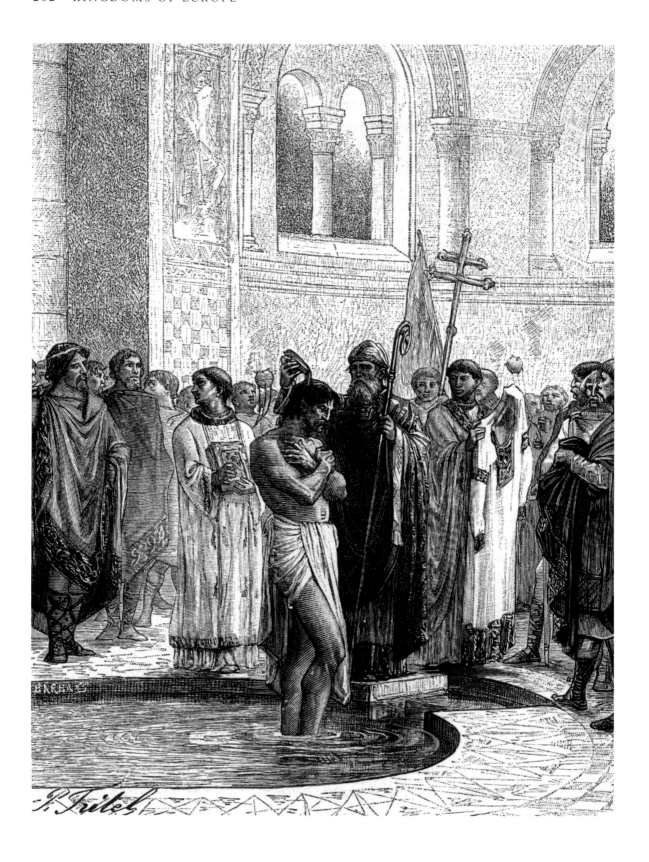

# LONDON BRIDGE IS FALLING DOWN

IT HAS BEEN SUGGESTED that the origin of the song 'London Bridge is Falling Down' lies in an attempt to deter or resist Norse raids by fortifying a bridge that was then demolished by a Norse fleet.

According to legend, ropes were attached to the bridge, which was then toppled by vigorous rowing aboard a large number of long ships. There is little to suggest this is true, however.

so Charles decided to co-opt them instead. In 911 he offered Rollo, leader of the Norsemen and probably a participant in the Siege of Paris, a belt of land along the coast. This would become Normandy and its Franco-Norse inhabitants the Normans.

Rollo became a Christian, at least officially, and took the name Robert when he became ruler of Normandy. His agreement with Charles the Simple did not prevent raiding elsewhere and, in Rollo's lifetime, his people probably changed little. However, Frankish influences took hold over time and within a century the Normans would come to resemble Franks more than Norsemen.

> FRANKISH INFLUENCES TOOK HOLD OVER TIME AND WITHIN A CENTURY THE NORMANS WOULD COME TO RESEMBLE FRANKS MORE THAN NORSEMEN.

## SCANDINAVIAN KINGDOMS

The Norse lands of 950 were very different from those of 800. Religious changes and the creation of larger social structures had altered the character of society. This permitted the creation of large forces such as the Great Heathen Army, but at the same time the Norsemen were losing their original character. In 800 they might have been described as sea-going adventurer barbarians, but by 950 they were becoming early medieval kingdoms whose politics resembled those of other civilized realms.

King Haakon of Norway faced numerous challenges from the sons of the deposed Eric Bloodaxe, and was mortally wounded in 961. He was succeeded by Harald Greycloak, son of Eric

OPPOSITE: The baptism of Rollo took place a year after his installation as duke of Normandy in AD 911. It marked the beginning of a transition from opportunistic Norse raiders.

Bloodaxe. At the time, Denmark was ruled by Harald Bluetooth, who lent support to Greycloak as he struggled to control his diminished realm. This enabled Greycloak to rebuild his power base, breaking away from the support of the Danish king.

Harald Bluetooth chose to support Haakon Sigurdsson, one of Greycloak's rivals, who assassinated Harald Greycloak and became king of Norway. In return for Bluetooth's support,

RIGHT: King Haakon of Norway was mortally wounded in battle on the island of Fitjar in AD 961. His reign was repeatedly challenged by the sons of Eric Bloodaxe, including Harald Greycloak.

Haakon subordinated himself, making Harald Bluetooth king
of a unified Scandinavia. He had converted to Christianity in
around 960, making Scandinavia (nominally at least) Christian.
His reign over Norway was short, ending after defeats suffered in
974 greatly reduced his power. In around 986 Harald Bluetooth
was deposed by his son Sweyn Forkbeard.

Sweyn financed his realm by attacking England and then
accepting Danegeld to stop, and increased his control over
Norway. In 1013 he invaded England, defeating King Aethelred
the Unready and briefly became king of England. He died just
weeks before his coronation, creating a confused situation that

ABOVE: The death of
Edward the Confessor, at
a time when there were no
clear rules for succession,
resulted in a three-way
fight for domination of
England. The Norman
victory marked the passing
of the old orders of Norse
and Anglo-Saxon power
and the beginning of a
new era.

eventually resulted in his sons becoming kings of parts of his
realm. Harald was crowned king of Denmark and Cnut (Canute)
king of England.

Cnut was succeeded in England by his sons Harald Harefoot
and then Harthacnut, after which rulership passed back to the
previous line of Aethelred the Unready. This placed the pious
Edward, known as the Confessor, on the throne of England.
Edward had no children and no clear heir, and his death would
bring about the tumultuous events of 1066.

## FEUDALISM

The feudal system grew out of the hierarchy of loyalties found
in earlier tribal societies. In theory, each social stratum had

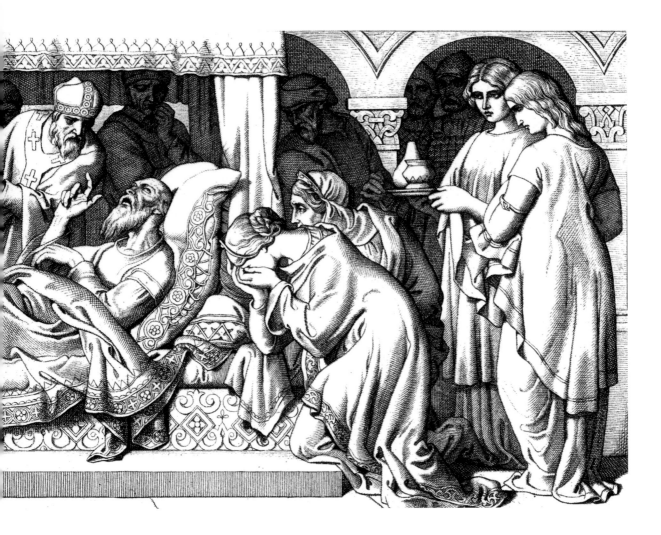

obligations to those both above and below it. The upper echelons of society were, for the most part, warriors, with craftsmen and merchants below them and the labouring classes at the bottom of the social pyramid. Near-absolute power was invested in the nobility and the king; the only restraint was the threat of rebellion or a challenge from an equally powerful noble.

WORDS FOR NOBILITY, SUCH AS CHEVALIER OR RITTER, ARE DERIVED FROM HORSE OWNERSHIP, BUT THE CONCEPT OF CHIVALRY HAD NOT BEEN INVENTED.

One of the primary status symbols of the period was a horse. Many words for nobility, such as chevalier or Ritter, are derived from horse ownership, but the concept of chivalry had not been invented. Chivalry in this era meant little more than possessing

BELOW: Feudalism grew out of the less formal tribal hierarchy, creating defined social strata. Ceremony and tradition began to disguise the origins of the medieval realms, which had been won by force of arms rather than any noble heritage or divine entitlement.

a horse, although there were expectations within the feudal system. A mounted warrior had status and was expected to be courageous, reliable and loyal. These would eventually develop into the knightly ideas of the High Middle Ages.

The feudal system reduced the financial burden of military forces on the central treasury by creating a warrior class that were also rulers of small territories. A fief would, in theory, generate enough income to support its lord, who had an obligation to serve when his superiors commanded it. This small proportion of fighting men was supported by other forces raised at need. Some might be professionals; less well equipped than the nobility but experienced and generally skilful.

Others were raised as needed and might be poorly equipped, unskilled or both. However, this was an age of warlords and post-tribal societies in which the ordinary farmer or townsman might have had to fight on several occasions. Weapon skills were passed on from one generation to the next in tribal society and that tradition had not died out. Thus the character of the early feudal armies fell somewhere in between the tribal hosts of the Volkswanderung era and the medieval armies of the next centuries.

# PRIMOGENITURE

THE SMOOTH TRANSITION OF power on the death or retirement of a ruler was important to the stability and well-being of any realm. Many tribal societies had a tradition of electing a new king from eligible candidates or crowning an heir as co-ruler in the latter years of the current king's life. This system had merits, as it allowed a prince to learn rulership under the tutelage of an experienced sovereign. In Anglo-Saxon England, it was not uncommon for an heir to be given a region to rule as sub-king, preparing him for the day he would be king in his own right.

Formal rules for succession did not exist in many societies during the Dark Ages. The earliest known set of rules originated with the Salian Franks, who lived near the Rhine. They practised agnatic primogeniture, whereby the crown passed to the eldest male child of the ruler. If no son existed, the nearest male relative was chosen – ignoring females even if they were much more closely related. In the event that a ruling line had died out, tracing back through previous generations would identify a 'cadet' branch of the family, who would then be elevated to ruling status. Only in the event that no suitable male candidate could be found would a female ruler be considered.

Agnatic, or Salic, primogeniture became common in the Middle Ages, although the strict rules of succession might be over-ruled by necessity or a candidate be passed over in favour of someone more suitable or more acceptable to the powerful nobles of the realm.

The practice of crowning an heir as co-ruler, as Charlemagne did with his son Louis the Pious, removed doubts about succession and allowed the future king to begin learning the business of rulership.

## THE NORMANS

The Norse leader Rollo took the name Robert and married into the Frankish royal family when he was granted Normandy by Charles the Simple. He did not use the term duke of Normandy and was not, in truth, a Frankish aristocrat in anything more than name. He did uphold the rule of law with great enthusiasm, though. Rollo was prone to mete out harsh punishments for relatively petty offences and reformed the local code of law into something stricter than the rather loose Frankish one he had inherited. His laws emphasized personal responsibility and a duty to observe honourable conduct.

Rollo retired in 927 and died soon afterward, leaving Normandy to his son William Longsword. William's son, Richard I of Normandy, was the first to use the title of duke. In his reign, the duchy was organized along feudal lines, which became the norm thereafter. His daughter, Emma of Normandy, married the English king Aethelred and, after his death, Cnut. Her son Edward eventually succeeded Cnut, becoming the last Anglo-Saxon king of England.

Richard I of Normandy died in 996, when he was succeeded by his young son Richard II. Normandy was by this point heavily involved in the politics of France and Europe in general. Relations with France, now ruled by the Capet dynasty, were good; Normandy assisted the king of France in his attempts to gain control over the Duchy of Burgundy. Richard II also gave

BELOW: **William I of Normandy, often known as William Longsword, expanded his realm both by conquest and by extracting concessions from Louis IV of France. He allied with Hugh the Great in rebellion against the Frankish throne but retained his duchy after a negotiated end to the conflict.**

refuge to the deposed Aethelred of England and his sons.

Richard II was succeeded in 1026 by his son Richard III, who was forced to put down a revolt by his brother Robert. Richard died soon after the end of the rebellion, passing the duchy to Robert. Normandy was at this time beset by internal troubles, some of which had begun as a result of the conflict between Richard and Robert. In the meantime, Norman adventurers were carving out realms for themselves in Italy. Accounts differ of how this conflict began, but it seems that Norman warriors became involved in Italian politics while passing on their way to and from the Holy Land. The Crusades were many years in the future at this point, but pilgrimages to Jerusalem and other holy sites were popular with nobles either as a means to win the favour of the Church or out of genuine devotion.

Norman involvement in Italy increased gradually, eventually leading to the creation of a Norman kingdom of Sicily and large holdings in southern Italy. In 1035, when Robert I of Normandy died, Italy was a land of opportunity and adventure. However, Robert's successor William had troubles nearer home. As an illegitimate child, there were disputes over his succession to the throne of Normandy and he was forced to consolidate his

ABOVE: Duke Robert of Normandy is sometimes known as 'the Magnificent'. He was accused of poisoning his brother to take the title of duke, gaining him the alternative nickname 'Robert the Devil'.

ABOVE: The assumption
of divine favour gave
legitimacy to the rulers
of the early medieval
world. Here Roger II of
Normandy is depicted
being crowned by Jesus
Christ himself.

power by a series of military campaigns. It was
not until 1047 that William was secure in his
position as duke of Normandy.

## THE SUCCESSION CRISIS IN ENGLAND

The English king, Edward the Confessor, did
not produce any children. It has been suggested
that he was so pious that he took a vow of
chastity, but this remains doubtful. Be that
as it may, he had to provide for succession in
some other way. William of Normandy was an
obvious candidate; he was related to Edward
and his duchy had provided shelter after the
deposition of Aethelred. William claimed that
Edward the Confessor had nominated him as
successor in 1051, although others challenged
this assertion. Edward's father-in-law was
Godwin, earl of Wessex. Such was his power
that, although exiled by Edward in 1051, he
simply returned and demanded to be reinstated. Although the
marriage of his daughter Edith to Edward had not produced the
hoped-for royal heir, Godwin had ambitions to place his son
Harold Godwinson on the throne of England.

The third contender was Tostig, younger son of Godwin and
a bitter enemy of Harold. Tostig had gone into exile with his
father and returned with him, becoming earl of Northumbria.
His harshness as a ruler resulted in a rebellion, forcing him to
flee in 1065. Tostig offered his services to William of Normandy
but then threw in with Harald Hardrada of Norway. Together,
they planned an invasion of England that would place Tostig on
the throne.

Edward the Confessor died in 1066. It is possible that he
favoured Duke William of Normandy as his successor – his
preference for filling his court with Normans had annoyed
many English nobles and he was well disposed towards William.
Whatever Edward's wishes might have been, Harold Godwinson
was proclaimed king of England on 6 January 1066.

Harold was aware that his reign would be challenged and made what preparations he could. The earliest Duke William was likely to be able to invade would be May, so Harold raised forces in the south of England and readied his fleet. Meanwhile, Tostig and Harald Hardrada began raiding the eastern coasts, eventually landing in Northumbria during September. Defeating local forces, they took York and began establishing themselves.

Time was an issue for Harold Godwinson. Most of his warriors could only be away from their farms for a few weeks or months. A ruler might or might not care about the welfare of his people, but trying to keep an army in the field for too long could ruin the harvest and cause a rebellion. The defensive force in the south had to be stood down for lack of supplies, opening the way for William to invade. Thus Harold's only viable strategy was to strike hard against Tostig and then turn to face William.

The first part of the plan went well. Harold's force came upon the invaders at Stamford Bridge in Yorkshire, inflicting a heavy defeat in which both Harald Hardrada and Tostig were killed. The remnants of their force returned to its ships and departed, freeing Harold to march southwards against William's army.

William of Normandy landed in England on 28 September 1066, three days after Harold's victory. William was a careful

BELOW: Upon the death of Edward the Confessor, Harold Godwinson was crowned king of England with almost indecent haste. Holding a coronation the day after Edward's death was seen by some as proof that Harold was grabbing power rather than succeeding according to the wishes of Edward.

and pragmatic ruler and commander, willing to withdraw if his position was compromised. He proceeded carefully, constructing forts to protect his supply line, and found himself confronting Harold's army on 14 October.

Harold's army was similar in many ways to the one it had defeated in September; a core of professionals armed with long-handled axes and large shields supported by a much larger body of spearmen lacking much in the way of armour. Arrayed in a shield wall formation, this was a powerful infantry force but it lacked mobility and the ability to strike at a distance. To a great extent this was an army from an era that was now passing.

THE NORMANS WOULD FACE REBELLIONS AND LOCAL RESISTANCE, BUT ULTIMATELY THEY WOULD BECOME MASTERS OF ENGLAND.

William's army, on the other hand, contained infantry, archers and cavalry and was capable of combined-arms co-operation. Despite this, the initial attack on Harold's line achieved little. Arrows caused few casualties among warriors well protected by their shield wall and the supply of missiles soon ran short. Most opponents would have archers of their own, with arrows shot back and forth as they were gathered from the ground. The English lack of archers became an

BELOW: Harold Godwinson's victory over invading Norsemen led by Harald Hardrada was a major triumph, but is overshadowed by his defeat a few weeks later at Hastings.

advantage of sorts. The English shield wall held against infantry and cavalry assaults for most of the day, and was broken by the English themselves. According to legend, William's cavalry made a feigned retreat to draw the English out of their defensive position. Once their ranks were opened, a renewed charge broke through. However, it is highly unlikely that this was a deliberate stratagem. A feigned retreat and subsequent rally to charge pursuers is extremely difficult to execute. It is more likely that a cavalry attack was repulsed, probably in some disorder, and that the retreat was genuine – at least until the English were counter-attacked by other forces.

ABOVE: The Bayeux Tapestry states that 'King Harold is Killed' but it is not clear whether the individual receiving an arrow in the eye or the one felled by a sword stroke – or both – represent the king of England.

Be that as it may, some elements of the English force did break ranks and were roughly handled, but the remainder fought on until Harold was killed. The nature of his death is debatable – the Bayeux Tapestry depicts the incident in an ambiguous manner – but whether he was killed with a sword or an arrow in the eye, or suffered both, is less important than the fact that Harold was slain. In an age of charismatic leadership, such a setback could cause a force to collapse – indeed, rumours that William had been killed had caused morale to plummet in the Norman Army earlier in the day. With their king dead, the English lost heart and began to retreat. Many died in the pursuit, although some elements of the English Army seem to have given good account for themselves in a rearguard action.

With Harold's army defeated, no significant opposition remained to William's conquest of Britain. The Normans would face rebellions and local resistance, but ultimately they would become masters of England. The army that completed the conquest was cast in the mould of a new era, with armoured cavalry as the

# THE BAYEUX TAPESTRY

MUCH OF WHAT IS known about the Norman Conquest comes from the Bayeux Tapestry, a rich yet cryptic source of visual information. It is not possible to say for sure which figure depicted as the slain King Harold is actually him. It could be both, either one, or perhaps neither. Thus although the idea that Harold was killed by an arrow in the eye is widely believed as fact, the reality is that we cannot know for sure. This lack of accurate written records is what characterizes a Dark Age and makes it extremely difficult to determine exactly what happened, to whom and when.

The Bayeux Tapestry presents a record – albeit one that is difficult to decipher – of events that took place a thousand years ago.

primary striking arm and other troops in support. This would be the shape of warfare for the next few hundred years.

The Norman conquest spelled the end of an era and the emergence of a new order all across Europe; an age of castle-building and strict rules of feudal succession; of grand cathedrals and royal dynasties. The warrior kings of the Dark Ages would give way to subtler rulers who demonstrated their power through the patronage of arts as well as military might.

## THE LEGACY OF THE DARK AGES

The so-called 'Dark Ages' were a period of transition from the collapse of the Roman Empire to the emergence of a new, feudal Europe. The term is apt in its strictest sense – few writings exist so information is patchy at best – but this is not the same thing as an era of violence and wanton destruction. There was conflict, of course – some of it traumatic to whole regions – but this was also a time of growth and development.

During the Dark Ages, Europeans discovered Iceland, Greenland and crossed the Atlantic Ocean to stand, albeit briefly, upon a distant continent. The two great religions – Christianity and Islam – developed into the beginnings of their modern form and established the regions they would dominate. Great works were undertaken; cathedrals were built and road networks that still exist today were constructed.

By the end of the Dark Ages, Europe had moved from a tribal social structure to a feudal one, with organized kingdoms linked by formal treaties. In these kingdoms of a thousand years ago lie the beginnings of modern countries such as France, Denmark, Sweden and England. We have tantalizingly few details available to us, but what we do know is that this was an age of endeavour and discovery rather than destruction. It began in chaos but ended in a new order, marking the passing of antiquity and the beginning of the medieval period.

Britain would never again be successfully invaded; the papacy would continue to lead the Catholic Church into modern times and France would be a power in European events for the next thousand years. Institutions and polities established in the Dark Ages have survived to the present day, making this period significant as the very beginning of the modern world.

WE HAVE FEW DETAILS AVAILABLE TO US, BUT WHAT WE DO KNOW IS THAT THIS WAS AN AGE OF ENDEAVOUR AND DISCOVERY RATHER THAN DESTRUCTION.

BELOW: A fourteenth-century miniature depicting a king and his knights. Society had changed since the fall of Rome, but a medieval ruler still needed to be a warrior as well as a statesman.

# Bibliography

Anonymous,
*The Anglo-Saxon Chronicle*
(Echo Library)

Brooke, Christopher,
*The Saxon and Norman Kings*
(Wiley-Blackwell, 2001)

Brown, Peter RL.,
*The World of Late Antiquity*
(WW Norton & Company, 1989)

Brown, Peter RL.,
*The Rise of Western Christendom: Triumph & Diversity 200–1000*
(Wiley-Blackwell, 2013)

Cantor, Norman F.,
*The Civilization of the Middle Ages*
(Harper Perennial, 1994)

Gibbon, Edward,
*The History of the Decline and Fall of the Roman Empire*
(Everyman's Library, 2000)

Halsall, Guy,
*Barbarian Migrations and the Roman West*
(Cambridge University Press, 2008)

Kelly, Christopher,
*The End of Empire: Attila the Hun and the Fall of Rome*
(WW Norton & Company, 2010)

Oman, Charles,
*The Dark Ages 476-918 AD*
(Independently published, 2017)

Wood, Ian N.,
*The Merovingian Kingdoms*
(Routledge (1993)

Wood, Michael,
*In Search of the Dark Ages*
(BBC Books, 2006)

Stenton, F.M.,
*Anglo-Saxon England*
(Oxford University Press, 2001)

# Index

Page numbers in bold refer to illustration captions

# PICTURE CREDITS

**AKG Images:** 18 & 19 (Peter Connolly)

**Alamy:** 15 (Granger Historical Picture Archive), 16 (Interfoto), 22 (Ancient Art & Architecture), 25 (Interfoto), 27 (Science History Images), 28 (Chronicle), 29 (Bildagentur-online), 31 (Pictorial Press), 34 (Classic Image), 36 (Interfoto), 37 (Falkensteinfoto), 38 (James Nesterwitz), 40 (North Wind Picture Archives), 41 (Classic Image), 42 (Artokoloro Quint Lox), 43 (Classic Image), 44 (Oldtime), 45 & 46 (Chronicle), 47 & 49 (The Picture Art Collection), 51 (Yolanda Perera Sanchez), 52 (Artefact), 56 (lunstream), 57 (Prisma Archivo), 59 (Austrian National Library/Interfoto), 61 (Lanmas), 63 (World History Archive), 65 Lanmas, 66 (Picture Art Collection), 68 (Interfoto), 69 (Chronicle), 72 (Artokoloro), 74 (Picture Art Collection), 75 (Lanmas),  77 (Classic Image), 79 (Lebrecht Music & Arts), 84 (GL Archive), 86 (De Luan), 87 (Classic Image), 91 (Chronicle), 93 (Chronicle), 94 (Walker Art Gallery), 99 left (Timewatch Images), 100 (Classic Images), 101 (Florilegius), 102 (Ian Dagnall), 104 (19thera), 107 & 109 (Chronicle), 111 (N J Murray), 112 (Sonia Halliday Photo Library), 113 (World History Archive), 114 (bilwissedition Ltd & Co. KG), 119 (Chronicle), 120 (Incamerastock), 121 (Historical Images Archive), 122 (Chris Hellier), 126 (Chronicle), 127 (Granger Historical Picture Archive), 128 (Niday Picture Library), 129 (Ian Dagnall), 131 (Godong), 132 (Chronicle), 133 (Granger Historical Picture Archive), 134 (Yolanda Perera Sanchez), 135 (DV Travel), 137 (Chronicle), 139 (Michael Sayles), 140 (Chronicle), 141 (imageBROKER), 143 (Prisma Archivo), 144 (De Luan), 145 (Barry Vincent), 146 (age footstock), 148 (Joris Van Ostaeyen), 153 (Granger Historical Picture Archive), 158 (Lars S. Madsen), 159 (Interfoto), 161-163 all (Prisma Archivo), 164 (Chris Hellier), 166 (Artokoloro Quint Lox Limited), 167 (Minden Pictures), 168 (Falkensteinfoto), 169 (National Geographic Image Collection 177 (Charles Walker Collection), 178 (AF Fotografie), 179 (Niels Quist), 183 (Mark A Schneider/Dembinsky Photo Associates), 185 (Interfoto), 187 (National Geographic Image Collection), 189 (parkerphotography), 191 (Prisma Archivo), 194 & 195 (Falkensteinfoto), 196 (NPC Collectiom), 198 (Photo 12), 201 (Nigel Reed QEDimages), 202 (Interfoto), 205 (Historical Images Archive), 206/207 (World History Archive), 210 (Glenn Harper), 211 (Yolanda Perera Sanchez), 212 (imageBROKER), 213 (Timewatch Images), 214 (Chronicle), 215 (GL Archive), 216 (Yagil Henkin), 217 (Universal Images Group North America LLC)

**Alamy/Heritage Image** Partnership: 6, 21, 58, 60, 78, 88, 151,152, 156, 160, 165, 172, 173, 175, 186, 190, 204, 209

**Amber Books/Art Tech:** 197

**Bridgeman Images:** 8 (Look & Learn), 9 (DeAgostini/Museo della Civilta Romana), 10 (Look & Learn), 11 (Musee d'Orsay), 12 (Severino Baraldi), 14 (Bridgeman), 32 & 33 (Biblioteca Estense), 50 (Look & Learn), 70 (DeAgostini /Icas94), 83, 85, 90, 95 & 97 all (Look & Learn), 98 (The Stapleton Collection), 116 (Look & Learn), 117 (The Stapleton Collection), 150 (Biblioteque Nationale, Paris, France), 170 (The Stapleton Collection), 174 (Biblioteque des Arts Decoratifs, Paris/France/Archives Charmet), 180 (De Agostini Picture Library), 184 (Bridgeman), 192 (Bridgeman), 199 (De Agostini Picture Library), 200 (Look & Learn), 208 (Biblioteca Nazionale Marciana, Venice, Italy)

**Dreamstime:** 17 (Veniamin Krasov), 23 (Oleg Bannikov), 73 (Edoma), 115 (Timawe), 130 (Giedrius Blagnys), 136 (Daniel M. Cisilino), 138 (Gunold), 154/155 (Toni Genes), 188 (James Kirkikis)

**Getty Images:** 62 (Universal Images Group), 80 (PHAS), 89 (Heritage Images), 99 right (Hulton Archive), 110 (Bettmann), 124 (PHAS), 176 & 181 (Werner Forman), 182 G?rald Morand-Grahame)

**Photos.com:** 55

**Shutterstock:** 92 (Gail Johnson)